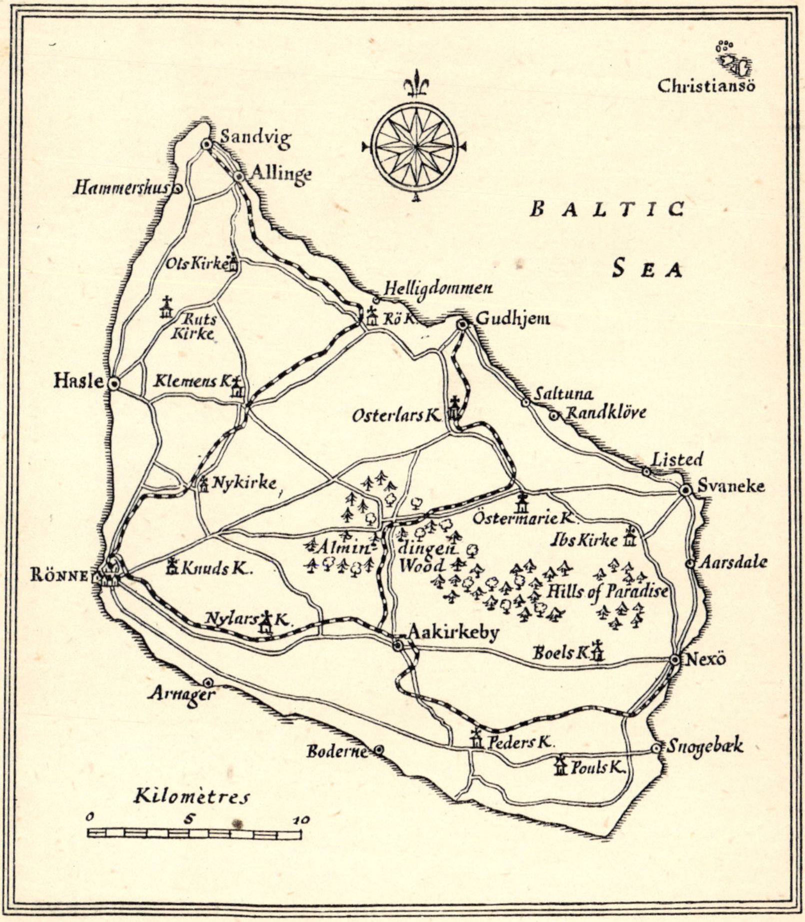

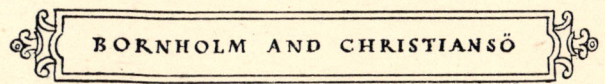

BORNHOLM AND CHRISTIANSÖ

226513

DL Baerlein
271   Baltic paradise.
B7
B3
1944

DATE DUE

JAN 12 1992			
MAR 07 2001			
NOV 10 2003			

Subject To Recall After 2 Weeks
LIBRARY
NORTH DAKOTA
STATE UNIVERSITY
FARGO, NORTH DAKOTA

DEMCO

BALTIC PARADISE

WARREN D. KRESS
O-17976 €3

BALTIC PARADISE

by
HENRY BAERLEIN

LONDON
FREDERICK MULLER LTD.
29 Great James Street, W.C.1

FIRST PUBLISHED BY FREDERICK MULLER LTD.
IN 1943
PRINTED IN GREAT BRITAIN
BY BUTLER & TANNER LTD.
FROME AND LONDON

LIST OF ILLUSTRATIONS

	Facing page
A View of Rönne, the Island Capital showing the Parish Church and part of the Harbour	42
One of Bornholm's Mediaeval Round Churches : these curious Structures served a Double Purpose, for Religious Service and as a Sanctuary in the event of a Pirate Invasion	43
A Stretch of the Road which runs across the Island	43
Osterlars Church—Exterior and Interior	58
Rocky Coast in the north-west of the Island	59
The Ruined Castle of Hammershus, dating from the 12th Century	59
Christiansö, the Harbour and Town	90
The Bridge connecting Christiansö (in the foreground) with Frederiksö, whose Fortress Tower is seen to the right	90
Gudhjem, the Harbour	91
Helligdommen, the famous Sanctuary Cliff	91
Svaneke, the little Port	106
The Smoking of Herrings on the Waterfront	106
Nylars Church, showing the Murals which are noted for their fine Colour Combinations, the Decorative Borders being particularly attractive. The Artist's technique, however, is primitive and his religious conceptions naïf	107
Nylars Church, dating from the 12th Century	107

Reproduced from photographs supplied by the Exclusive News Agency

THE DANES IN THIS WAR

THEIR TRADITION   Everyone has heard of Nelson's blind eye at Copenhagen, but not everyone in Britain knows of something which, during the engagement, he gazed at with the greatest interest. He was being fought by so tiny a ship that one had almost to bend over the bulwarks in order to see her. And that night when Nelson dined with the Prince Regent he begged him to promote this very gallant young officer, whose birthplace is the little port of Assens, at no vast distance from Odense, the capital of the island of Fyn. Along the winding, cobbled streets of Odense the pilgrims come to the cottage of a poor shoe-repairer whose son was Hans Andersen; there is at the birthplace of Willemoes at Assens merely a blue tablet on the outer wall of quite a stately house and the pilgrims are few in number. " If I were to promote this young man for his gallant behaviour," said the Prince Regent, " then I would have to promote them all." There will be some who will apply to his conduct during the bombardment the words of Cyrano de Bergerac, who exclaimed, as he defied his hostile fate: " *Non, non, c'est bien plus beau lorsque c'est inutile.*" But such bravery, whether useless or not, has been repeated over and over again in the present war by his compatriots.

Escapist literature is all very well and there are persons who may enjoy to read the story of an expedition round a Danish island in the years of peace. But if they come to have a liking for that island and several of its inhabitants they will desire to know what has been done in less pacific times by members of that little nation. Willemoes can sleep untroubled in his grave.

* * *

THE SEA IS IN THEIR BLOOD   It was unbelievable to anyone who knows the Danes that they would have been content to remain under the Nazis if any other course was open to them; and when their country was invaded and the German-controlled radio from Denmark ordered them to proceed to a neutral port and the B.B.C. recommended the Danes all over the world to throw in their lot with us, the overwhelming majority made for some Allied harbour.

There was an exception, a captain who, without consulting his officers or crew, decided to obey the Germans. At a meeting on board it was unanimously settled that the captain should be locked into his cabin. And when the ship was brought into a South Wales port he charged the men with mutiny and the local authorities locked them up. There was at the time no Danish Seamen's Union over here, but that of the Norwegians intervened. The facts were explained, the men were liberated and the captain exchanged places with them.

Not only were the Danish seamen without a Union in this country, they had not, like the Dutch, the Norwegians and the others, a Government of their own to support them here. But the Ministry of Shipping took these friends of ours—Allies in all but the name—under its wing and at a certain port Sir Arthur Salter of that Ministry opened for them a very pleasant club where between voyages they can rest awhile, meet their old companions, obtain (at cost price) food prepared in the Danish fashion, read Danish papers, and so on. A good many of these men have quite a fair command of English, which they learned at school. One of them told me that he sailed in English and French ships solely in order to perfect himself in those languages. And as one talks with them the loudspeaker announces that on such-and-such a ship a second engineer is wanted, on another ship two deck-hands, and so on.

The Germans have been declaring over the air that Britain has seized all these Danish ships—and it will probably come as a surprise to many when they learn that more than 500,000 tons of Danish shipping, which includes their largest and most up-to-date vessels, that is to say about half the total tonnage of the Danish merchant navy, is now serving under the Red Ensign—but, of course, those who man these ships, chiefly Danes, know very well that a most careful account is kept of the earnings of the vessels, which will be handed over to the owners after the war.

ALLIES IN ALL BUT NAME

It is not generally realized how much a seaman of a neutral country was paid, especially if his ship did not sail in convoy (though many a Danish owner turned a blind eye on this and asked no questions, so that officially he did not know that the convoying method had been adopted, despite German threats, and he paid as if it had not been). On such a ship an ordinary seaman received as much as £50 a month and it is noteworthy that there are no heart-burnings on this account. "What we like," said a blond young man, and I found that his opinion was shared by all of them, " is to be the same as the British are. In the last war we only made money. But now it is much better. It is a grand thing to be on the right side, to be giving our help as we are doing."

* * *

HOW SOME OF THEM CAME OVER

They have also given their lives. No less than 450 of them were drowned when the Germans, before the invasion of Denmark, were sinking neutral ships. "We reminded some Germans of that," said another of the men, " when they argued that we were not acting in accord with International Law. That was when my ship had taken refuge in a Norwegian fjord after the invasion and a German plane used to come every day and order us to go home. When it saw that we would not do this they bombed us and killed and wounded a few men and damaged the ship. So we took her, with the help of a local fisherman, far into the fjord under the side of a mountain where we were able to repair her. After that some Norwegian airmen arrived and said they would like to go with us to Britain. They told us about some German airmen who were interned in the neighbourhood; they had bombarded a place in England and, owing to engine-trouble, had to come down in Norway. Well, it was decided that these men should come over with us and be interned in Britain, which would be much better than leaving them in Norway. And when they accused us of breaking International Law we told them they had broken it a hundred times every day since September 1939."

"You see," said another young Dane, "we have a sea tradition in our country and we love to be with Britain now on that account. We are so busy—always on the way. We turn the ships round as quickly as we can. We remember that speech of Sir Arthur Salter; he said that a single ship can bring in a year as much wheat as can be grown in 30,000 acres, and four times a year she can bring as much petrol as will drive a fleet of lorries thirty million miles. So we are glad, you bet, to be helping."

"The captain of our ship," said a big, jovial fellow, "summoned us to a conference and asked what we wanted to do. Not a single man was for going back to German-controlled Denmark."

"That," I said, "was democratic of the captain."

"But he knew the answers beforehand. We are a people who have always had freedom."

Then a curly-headed sailor remarked that, on the subject of what is democratic, he might mention that some of his compatriots had joined the British Army, most of them in the Buffs, of which the King of Denmark is the honorary colonel. It was arranged that they should serve for a month and only stay on if they wished, while the British authorities were empowered to point out, after a month, that any of these men were unsuitable. And up to this day not one Dane who has chosen the Army has left it.

* * *

DIPLOMACY AT DAKAR AND IN WASHINGTON AND LONDON

A certain number of Danish merchantmen were interned at Dakar, because their crews objected to being repatriated to occupied Denmark, while their ships were to be taken to Marseilles and, no doubt, used by the Vichy Government. When

General de Gaulle and the British approached Dakar the port authorities placed a screen of Danish ships round the *Richelieu*, but that did not cause the Danes much anxiety because they knew that the British would avoid doing them any harm; and as a matter of fact the naval craft which so severely damaged the *Richelieu's* propeller dived under the Danish ships without touching them. " It was interesting in the town," said an alert young man. " The natives told us that they have a vote for a member of the French Parliament, but they envied the lot of their relatives farther down the coast in the British colonies, and they all said they would like to go with us if ever we thought of escaping; but there was not much room in the boat we were planning to capture. Meanwhile we noticed that when German officers went into the dining-room of the hotel the other people got up and walked out, except some of the French officers. And, at last, with two friends on a Sunday morning it was possible for me to set out in the boat when the mine-field was open. We pretended to be fishing and waited till the *Richelieu*—she could then only do nine knots—was a longish way from us. She was patrolling up and down. Luckily there came a wind and on the next afternoon we arrived at Gambia, where they treated us splendidly. The wife of the Governor could actually speak some Danish and she went shopping with us. Then we were taken to Sierra Leone and so to Britain."

It would be wrong to say that these men have no criticisms to make. They did not at all like the newspaper reports on the seizure of German, Italian and Danish ships in the United States, because it seemed that they were all classed together, whereas, of course, the Danes were only too anxious for the ships to be taken over and the last thing in the world they would have done was to damage them. Henrik Kauffmann, the Danish Minister in Washington, had made an agreement with regard to these ships. And when they were thus to be no longer left safely in harbour, but were henceforward to be exposed to all the risks of war, it came about that on the next day there was a rise in shipping shares on the Copenhagen bourse, to the undisguised fury of the Germans, for it indicated very plainly who, in the opinion of the Danes, were going to win this war. Something of the same kind happened at Diego Suarez in Madagascar, where the British General who occupied the town posted, as a precaution, an armed guard outside the banks, so that there should not be too great a rush of people wishing to withdraw their money. There was a rush, it was of people who, seeing that the hand of Vichy was no longer over Diego Suarez, desired to entrust the banks with their funds, for now their confidence had been restored.

Very courageous was another step taken by Mr. Kauffmann when he placed Greenland under the protection of the United States. He thus saved that country from being used by the Germans as a base for air operations directed against Iceland or Great Britain and, of course, Atlantic Shipping. Denmark's sovereignty is categorically recognized in the agreement, so that the colony will return absolutely to the Motherland after the war. It was only after the agreement had been signed that Mr. Kauffmann informed his Government that he had done this on behalf of King Christian, that it was in the best interests of Denmark and Greenland, and that he had acted in accordance with his conscience and his feelings of loyalty to his King. In reply he was immediately recalled; when he ignored this he was dismissed and it was announced that criminal investigations would be started against him, not only for flagrant disregard of his official duties but for jeopardizing the security of the State. Mr. Paul Palmér, a very well-informed Danish journalist, says in his book *Denmark in Nazi chains* that the Minister in Washington was very popular before this episode and that he had now become almost a national hero in Denmark. The German-dictated orders against him had the satisfactory effect of giving the Danes in their unhappy plight something to laugh at. Mr. Kauffmann's example was followed by various diplomatic and consular officials in North and South America, Iceland, Asia and so forth.

Immediately after the signing of the anti-Comintern Pact in Berlin by the then Danish Minister of Foreign Affairs, the Minister in London, Count Eduard Reventlow, sent a telegram to the Danish Legation in Stockholm to be forwarded to the Foreign Office in Copenhagen. This telegram stated that he had broken off relations with his home Government, since he was convinced that the signing of this Pact was " likely seriously to damage Denmark's reputation in Great Britain and to endanger the traditional good relations between Denmark and the British Commonwealth." This step was no surprise to the British Government, who saw, moreover, that the whole staff of the Legation, as well as the Consuls in the provincial towns, were backing the Minister's decision. He will remain at his post in London as the envoy of King Christian. In an article written by Count Reventlow in June 1942, on the occasion of the thirtieth anniversary of the King's accession, he said that " the main reason the King's influence has been so deeply felt is that his relations with his people have been of such a close and intimate character that each Dane, in his peculiar way, feels that there is a personal relationship between him and his King. And so his loyalty as a subject is naturally bound up with his devotion to and admiration for the King."

* * *

HOW KING CHRISTIAN HAS INSPIRED THEM

The Danes are a people who glory in their democratic King. That was always his way of life. During his father's reign he had to take his turn at sentry-go outside the palace, and when, as King, he went motoring about the country he would often stop at some cottage and ask if an old acquaintance of his was at home. He detests formality and a peasant will very soon be talking to him as man to man. An amusing example occurred not long ago when a farmer in Jutland complained to him of the weight of taxation. He did not see why he should be obliged to pay for this and that. And after the King had patiently explained to him the whole system the farmer agreed that he had been mistaken and he realized that he was not, after all, paying for what he thought he should not pay.

The dignified and unceasing resistance of the King has been a vast encouragement to his people. One morning while he was having his usual ride through the streets of Copenhagen, unaccompanied either by aide-de-camp or servant, he noticed that a German flag was flying from a building where it had no business to be. He beckoned to a German officer and requested him to have the flag removed; the officer murmured something about superior orders. " If the flag is not taken down in an hour when I shall be returning from my ride," said the King, " a Danish officer will haul it down."—" That Danish officer," exclaimed the Nazi, " will be shot ! "—" That Danish officer," said the King, " will be I." And when he came back from his ride the flag had vanished.

When the German Minister expressed the Fuehrer's hopes that there would be no more delay in the introduction of anti-Semitic legislation and that Danish Jews would be ordered to wear an armlet with a yellow star, the King said : " If the Danes will have to wear a yellow star then the Royal Family will wear it like the rest of them."—" But—but," spluttered the Minister, " I didn't say all the Danes, I said——"—" Excuse me," said the King, " my people are the Danes. Their religion is their own concern."

A few days later it came to the knowledge of the King that there was to be a special celebration in the synagogue, and he immediately informed the Chief Rabbi that he would be present. He arrived in full-dress uniform with a Sovereign's escort, and attended the ceremony to the undisguised horror of the Germans.

(Look upon this picture and on that : here was the King of a small and defenceless country refusing, for it is civilized, to comply with Berlin's Jewish demands. In Vichy France, much larger and then in control of a fleet and an Empire, anyone striving to secure a position of power was ready to outvie his competitors in offering a brutal Jewish programme to win the favour of Berlin. When the Papal Nuncio, Monsignor Valeri, protested against the extreme terror of these persecutions Pétain interrupted him: "An unfortunate subject!" he exclaimed. "The Pope understands me and approves my attitude."—"That," replied Valeri, "is a fundamental error. In this matter the Holy Father neither understands nor approves." Pétain caused his friend M. Barthélémy, member of the Vichy Cabinet, to write an article in *Patrie*, an extravagantly got-up paper published in Algiers, in which he stated that the Jews had not fully become a part of the French body politic. And yet it was for their Patrie that thousands of them gave their lives in the Great War. This sorry spokesman of the Marshal went on to say that there would be exemptions, such as "the great Bergson, an indisputable ornament to French literature and philosophy." He might have added that Bergson was proud enough to refuse this exemption and if France had possessed such a leader as King Christian instead of a Laval who personally enriched himself very considerably from the spoils of Jewish property, which was at his disposal after he had delivered the owners to the Gestapo or drafted them to the heaviest type of forced labour on the Trans-Sahara railway or incarcerated them in a "criminal camp" at Bendonit in French Morocco, regardless of whether they had an American visa and steamship passage, regardless of the age limit and of the fact that in their fight for a better France many of them had been decorated—but it is futile to compare a country like that of Pétain and Laval with King Christian and his people.)

What an inspiration to his people it has been to have such a King. When the German Minister sent a note asking for the "temporary right" to use eight Danish torpedo-boats, this was refused. The ships were seized and the Danish radio and Press were forbidden to say a word about it; but the King issued an Order of the Day to the Army and Navy giving all the details. No, King Christian has not endeared himself to the Germans. When they arrived it was with strict orders from home to behave in such a kindly fashion that other countries would long to have them as overlords. All that was wanted was cordial collaboration on the part of the Danes. But the oldest kingdom in Europe was not to be duped by the newest political charlatanism.

And the arch-charlatan, Hitler, is not very pleased with King Christian. When he congratulates someone on his birthday he expects that this will be acknowledged in the same sort of language as he has employed. Every year in May he has sent a hearty kind of message to King Christian; the King's reply was always the same: " Thanks. Christian Rex." Last year, to compel a less laconic answer, the Fuehrer's telegram was particularly effusive. And the King replied, " Thanks. Christian Rex."

* * *

THE RESISTANCE IN DENMARK
"Our ancestors would turn in their graves," said the *Aarhus Amtstidende*, an important provincial paper a couple of months after the German invasion, " if they were to see the gigantic police force which is at present thought necessary to supervise the Danish people." Their sentiments with regard to the Nazis can be seen from the fact that when the party of Frits Clausen, the Danish Nazi (formerly a general practitioner of Bovrup in South Jutland), presented itself at the 1932 elections to the Lower House, they received in the whole of Denmark a total of 757 votes. It has not been made known whether Clausen was consoled in that dark hour by a telegram from Sir Oswald Mosley, whose 23 candidates, it will be remembered, for Westminster were all defeated, all except two of them losing their deposits. More substantial assistance had been given to Clausen; and when, during the budget debate in November 1941, a member of the Lower House asked a question as to the source of the Danish Nazis' funds for their enormous newspaper and poster campaign, saying that at least a million crowns were involved, Clausen feebly replied that to suggest they received money from Germany

was an insult both to them and to Germany.[1] But Poul Jensen, the manager of their paper, *Fædrelandet*, never concealed the fact that the millions which it cost to run the paper came from foreign sources. When the Germans examined the results of all these efforts they must have wondered whether it was very wise to continue to throw away their cash. So very few of the stubborn Danes reacted favourably to their blandishments. It was in November 1940 that Clausen felt that, with pressure from the street, he could overthrow the Government. He planned a series of demonstrations intended to carry the provinces, and then on this popular wave he would march victoriously into Copenhagen. A worse miscalculation has never been made since Hitler's Munich Putsch. Clausen's initial demonstration at Haderslev in North Slesvig was a complete fiasco. The population, on learning what was afoot, swooped on the Nazis and beat them up, eagerly assisted by the police. Nazi reinforcements, drawn from other parts of the country, were driven off and in the end the police had to protect the Nazis against the loyal population. The King made no attempt to conceal where his sympathies lay; he sent personal greetings to policemen who had been wounded in the course of the conflict.

And what was the outlook round about them for the Danish people? Norway's gallant resistance, inspiring though it was, had been broken. Holland and Belgium were overrun, France had collapsed and the British Expeditionary Force had been withdrawn from the Continent. In their own country the Press and radio were muzzled; and yet it was difficult to kill the characteristic Danish wit. Thus the afternoon paper, *Ekstrabladet*, in Copenhagen once brought out an article with double spacing between the lines, which, so it explained, made it easier for the readers to read between them. But it was the inner resources, the

---

[1] When Clausen brought an action against a compatriot who had described him as the modern equivalent of Ulfeldt, the notorious traitor of the seventeenth century, the verdict was given for the defendant.

moral strength of an old democracy which carried Denmark through this period when darkness descended upon Europe. It has been pointed out by Mr. T. M. Terkelsen in his admirable pamphlet, " Denmark : Fight follows Surrender," how the population, stunned by the suddenness of the blow, awakened and cast aside the recommendation to live on comfortable terms with an all-powerful neighbour. Rather have they been inspired by the grand example of North Slesvig which fought against Prussian methods for three generations—and won. The glorious traditions of that ravaged province are now as a trumpet call to the whole country. Denmark will undoubtedly win again. But this will not come about because Danes hate Germans by instinct; it will be because the brook which separates Denmark and Germany separates two worlds. On the northern side is a Nordic race, by nature, by education and by history deeply democratic. To the south is another people, with another conception of life, with other ideals, biologically another race. The modern boast that Germans are a Nordic race has no foundation in facts, and it is to the genuine distress of the Nazis that the Nordic people refuse to accept them as brethren.

Radio and the Press may be muzzled in Denmark, but this merely shows the people that the Germans realize what kind of a people they are. They have their spokesmen, for instance Dr. la Cour and Arne Sørensen, who were sentenced on August 5th, 1941, at the Copenhagen Town Court to eighty and sixty days' imprisonment respectively for having published a pamphlet entitled " Words to us to-day," which was held as likely to damage Denmark's relationship with a foreign power. The pamphlet was confiscated and this same foreign power demanded that Dr. la Cour should be imprisoned after he had produced another pamphlet : " About saying Yes—and No." When King Christian received him and Arne Sørensen in audience there was a furious outburst in the Danish Nazi Press which charged the King with " abusing the Royal Powers." Dr. la Cour had cleverly adapted Fichte's speeches to the German people during the French occupation of Prussia—

and, by the way, what a world of difference there is between King Christian and Frederick-William III. " Not one of Napoleon's marshals," says Professor Tarlé,[1] "not one of his own brothers whom he had placed on the various European thrones was so grovelling, so panic-stricken in the presence of the Emperor as the Prussian King." Here is an extract from Fichte that was used by Dr. la Cour: " This humiliation at being unable to act freely, this bitterness at encountering spies everywhere, this vexation at the sight of occupation troops in all the streets of Berlin and the knowledge that they are strutting about in the same way in every town in Germany, on her roads and in her ports. . . . There was none other upon whom to set one's hope but England—that old, tough, fabulously slow and fabulously tenacious England—freedom's last bulwark ! Civilization's bulwark ! What a debt would one not owe to England—a German would never be able to forget that." Fichte was called by Alfred Rosenberg, Hitler's philosopher, " the pioneer of the Nazi movement " for having awakened Germany to national consciousness. But the Danes were not to be awakened.

When Napoleon was moving eastward across Germany in May 1812 he was conscious of being Europe's dictator in the fullest sense of the word. With German kings, dukes and princes rivalling one another in flattery and sycophancy, he would have thought it absurd to worry about Leipzig or Göttingen students singing patriotic songs in taverns or about the suspicious lectures of an obscure Professor Fichte. " When I first heard from Stuart of the *Courier*," says Coleridge in his Table Talk, " that Bonaparte had declared that the interests of small States must always succumb to great ones, I said : ' Thank God, he has sealed his fate ; from this moment his fall is certain.' " The Danes know that this was said when Napoleon's star was still at its zenith, but that the prediction came true. To-day they have their trust not only in others but in themselves, whether in the homeland or in the free world outside it.

[1] *Napoleon's Invasion of Russia—1812*, p. 24.

DANISH SEAMEN COME FROM SOUTH AMERICA   Let me tell you of a few other talks I have had with Danish seamen over here. "Well," said one of them, a man with a rugged, furrowed face, "my ship arrived at an Argentine port soon after Denmark had been invaded and we remained there for fourteen months. The other freedom-loving people, such as the Dutch, the Norwegians or the Yugoslavs, sailed in and out again; but we had not, as they had, a Government in London, and so we had not enough money to pay the harbour dues. Fortunately in that part of the Argentine a number of Danish farmers have settled down, and some of us went up there and worked on the land, which is good for growing grain."

"You got on well," I asked, "with the Argentine people?"

"Surely," he said. "In fact the only fight I ever saw there was between one party of Italians and another. You see we had Italian ships in the harbour, because they were afraid of running the British blockade. These men were mostly in favour of Mussolini; but the Italians who had established themselves on shore had been out of their country, most of them, for a long time and they said that Mussolini was leading it to disaster. They and the others fought with knives and it was a disaster for the sailors, of whom seven were taken to the hospital."

"You didn't meet any German sailors?" I asked.

"No," he said, "but every now and then a German ship came in to load grain; seventy-four German ships were seized by Brazil in the last war and a good many of them are still being used. We liked the Brazilians too—they take life easily, not exerting themselves very much, so that, for instance, a three-thousand-ton ship would usually have a crew of sixty men."

At this point another Dane, a handsome young man, broke into the conversation. He too had been rather stranded in the Argentine, but in his case it was due to the captain of the ship. "I will tell you how it was," he said. "The captain came from that part of Denmark which was

German until the end of the last war, and in that war he served in German ships. Then he became a Danish subject and swore to be loyal, and it seems they believed him. But in his heart he was still a German, and when he had the opportunity he showed it. In that harbour he treated us very badly, giving us hardly any money, so that we were in extreme distress. We therefore took the electric fans and other things out of the ship and sold them to Americans."

"Didn't the captain notice that?" I asked.

"He never came to our part of the ship," said the young man. "He was afraid of being hit on the head. He received money for us from the Danish farmers and, without telling us about it, sent it back, saying we had quite enough. For a long time he refused to let us have our papers, so that we could sign on in another ship, but the excellent Danish Minister in Washington sent him a telegram that he had to let a man have his discharge papers if he asked for them. And when I left the ship he had only two persons with him, a steward and a cook."

"The captain I have been sailing with," said another young man, "is just the opposite. He also came from that part of Denmark which was formerly German—it would be funny if he were born in the next house to the other man—and he always felt himself to be a good Dane. In the last war the Germans compelled him to serve in one of their U-boats, and now he is perfectly happy as the captain of one of our largest merchant ships."

* * *

THEY COME FROM SPAIN AND AFRICA

On another occasion when I had looked in at the Danish Club I happened to meet a little group of men who had been to Spain. One of them had been chief steward in various ships. "And in 1933," he said, "I fell in love with a Spanish girl in the south-east of that country. I married her and for the next few years I had a fruit farm and all was well. When the Spanish Civil War broke out of course all my sympathies were with the

Government side—and if most of the Spaniards had not been on that side Franco would not have had to bring in Moors to shoot down his fellow-Catholics. Anyhow, I joined the International Brigade. In November '36 we were in Madrid, holding it against the Italians, and we had scarcely any arms, so we seized a supply from the enemy, and Russia and Mexico sent us some. By the way, those Russian fighter planes were fine, the fastest I have ever seen. And talking of things that go fast, those Italians at Guadalajara ran over fifty-six kilometres in two days. We ran after them till we were tired and then we dug ourselves in. We found that the Italians are only useful if they outnumber the opposition by five to one."

" How did you get out of Spain in the end ? " I asked.

" We got into France and they disarmed us. I had some money hidden under my uniform, so I got civilian clothes and bought tickets for my wife and myself to Paris. Later on I took her to Oran in North Africa and there she is now. The people there can all talk Spanish, so she is fairly comfortable, but I am hoping to get her over here."

" Oran ! Oran ! " cried another seaman, a blond young fellow. " My ship was there when France went out of the war. We had to stay there some time, but at last five of us got hold of a lifeboat that belonged to the harbour. And one night, while the Frenchmen were asleep, we cut the ropes and rowed away. For six days we were at sea— we had plenty of water, but nothing to eat except a little bread and two tins of sardines. We used the oil of the sardines to light up our compass in the night and in the end we arrived at a place in Spain. The Danish Consul was very nice, he fixed it up for us to stay at a small hotel —the Spanish police had no objection. They asked us how we had got the boat, and we said we had bought it. Of course, we didn't want to return to Denmark while the Nazis were there, but the police didn't want us to leave in a British ship, so we fixed it up with those English people and "—he smiled happily as he told me this—" one day we swam out to the ship, leaving all our clothes and our papers in the little hotel. The crew of the ship fitted us out with other clothes and took us to Gibraltar and then another British ship brought us to England."

* * *

THEIR LIFE IS NOT MONOTONOUS

A variety of work falls to the lot of the four or five thousand Danish seamen sailing under the Red Ensign. I met three who had been in the Lofoten Islands expedition, when installations working for Germany were destroyed. "Our ship," they told me, "was the supply ship. We had on board all kinds of things for the inhabitants, and I can tell you they were glad to see us. The warships with us were British, Norwegian and Polish, also some Belgian soldiers—naturally on an expedition of that sort everyone wants to go, and I think the British authorities did their best to share it out among the Allies. We Danes, of course, are not officially called Allies, but the British say that makes no difference to the friendship that unites us. Well, the Lofoten people had not had any coffee or cigarettes for a long time, and soon the smell of coffee came out of every house and everyone seemed to be smoking all the time. We had cut the cable to the mainland and broken up the Germans' radio station, so that the Germans there could not send for help. We took them back to England and a lot of islanders—in my ship were 55, including a baby four months old. The only German from the mainland while we were there was a Heinckel, which always used to come over once a week, to see that everything was all right. That Heinckel was attended to all right and now it is at the bottom of the sea."

I asked if he had seen any quislings.

"I only saw one myself," he said, "but he didn't see me, because he was blindfolded when they brought him on board. I think he was the owner of the factory which had been working for the Nazis. He ran up into the hills when we came, but they caught him. Talking of quislings," he said, "a Norwegian friend of mine told me the other day about something which had happened to Quisling himself. He is very upset because of the great resistance to him in Norway, so that he has been trying to drown his anxieties in drink. When he was found 'drunk and disorderly' he was not punished, but when he was heard to say: 'God help me when England wins!' the Nazis punished him very severely."

One often has the greatest difficulty in getting these fine fellows to talk about the dangers they have gone through. But that is the way with seamen. Calm weather and storm, it is all a part of their life—I once met one in South America who had just been through a terrible week of tempests rounding the Horn, and when I asked him to tell me something about it he laughed and said he really couldn't remember anything that was worth talking about—it was all, he said, quite ordinary. And now they include in what they call "ordinary" their experiences in being bombed, torpedoed and drifting for two or three weeks on a raft. (But I must add that a good many appear to have been at sea throughout the war without seeing a single German U-boat or plane.) One day, however, I did get a little story out of a man whose ship was engaged by the *Scharnhorst* or the *Gneisenau*—he was not sure which—" Our ship," he said, " was fast for a cargo ship. Her usual speed was eighteen knots and we were not sailing in convoy. We were east of Newfoundland when the warship started firing at us. She had ten-inch guns, ours were only four-inch ones, but of course we answered back. It looked as if the German was going to ram us, so we threw away our passports and papers. In our hold was carbide, it started to burn and we had to abandon the ship. The boat I was in capsized, so I had to swim for three-quarters of an hour. Then a British warship, larger than the German, came up; so the German made off and we were rescued and taken to Iceland."

" And you are going to stay on the sea ? " I asked.

He looked surprised. " Of course I am," he said. " It is my life. And the British and Allied command of the sea will bring back our old free life to Denmark. That will be fine for the children. Just at present I am going to school."

Now it was my turn to be surprised.

"Here, in this port," he said, "they have started a school for Danes who want to become mates or engineers. Usually there are about fifteen of us at the school. The British helped us to set it up. The head of the school is a Dane who won the highest prize at the Danish Navigation School, and after four months we are examined. The examination is in English, but neither that nor the subjects cause us much trouble. Oh, I tell you it's a splendid life! When I go back to Denmark after the war my mother and father won't say that I have wasted my time, particularly if I then am a full-blown engineer."

* * *

DANISH AIRMEN ARE WITH US In April 1942 Mr. Churchill accepted a cheque for £38,300, collected by the comparatively small number of Danes abroad—and it would have been larger if those in the United States had not considered that their first duty lay with the land of their adoption now that she was also in the war. With the sum presented to Mr. Churchill Danish pilots were able to take the air, flying their own planes in a squadron of the R.A.F. One of their Spitfires was named after Niels Ebbesen, the Danish hero who, in 1340, killed Count Gert, the Commander of the German armies which had occupied Denmark; another fighter was called Valdemar Atterdag, after the Danish King who completed Niels Ebbesen's work by expelling the Germans and reuniting the Danish provinces; the name of the third machine was "Skagen ind," which means "Homeward bound through the Skaw," and that is the aim of all the officers and men of the Free Danish Merchant Navy who so generously contributed to the raising and arming of its own hopes on R.A.F. wings. Accepting the first Danish Fighter-Flight on behalf of the Commander-in-Chief R.A.F. an Air Commodore said that young Danes were now on their way to join the R.A.F. from all over the world. He emphasized that Danish pilots are second to none in the service; one of those who would fly these new machines had escaped from Denmark in the face of tremendous difficulties. "I am very glad," said Mr. Churchill, "that you have devoted your munificent and important contribution to the Air Force, because it is the part of our armed attack which is most constantly in contact with the enemy. . . . I have very little doubt that the day will come, perhaps sooner than it would be prudent or sensible to hope—the day will come when Denmark will be free from the grip in which she has been held and when she will resume her independent, honoured and ancient place among the free people and States of Europe."

Other Danish pilots are to be found among the Norwegian squadrons in this country and elsewhere, for there exist no linguistic obstacles between them. And no other obstacles—I happened to come across a Danish commanding officer with a number of his men, all of whom were Norwegians. Their ages were much the same and it was delightful to see on what terms they were with each other. The young Danish officer had only, he said, one regret, namely, that he could not provide me with such a supergood meal—but it was most satisfactory—as was given to some German airmen at a certain place on the Scandinavian coast, and they sat over it for so long that a couple of enterprising fellows (one of them was thereupon produced) seized the opportunity and the plane in which they reached Britain without any incident. There probably was some incident when the Germans had to report to their superiors, but that is a matter of surmise.

* * *

THE WORK OF THE DANISH COUNCIL

Seeing that the Danes, unlike our other friends, had no Government of their own in this country and it was necessary to co-ordinate their efforts, the Danish Council was formed in London in September 1940. The first Council was of necessity a self-appointed assembly, consisting of well-known Danes who had taken the lead in organizing this Movement. They chose by acclamation as President of the Danish Council, Mr. F. Krøyer-Kielberg, whose long and very successful business life in this country had never brought him to forget the country of his birth or to moderate the munificence—and now more than ever —with which he has supported every good work of his compatriots. It was subsequently felt that the influence of the Council would be strengthened if it were to consist of elected representatives freely chosen by the members of the Association of Free Danes, and in November 1941 a Council elected by free and secret ballot took over the management of the Free Danish Movement in Great Britain, under the continued leadership of Mr. Krøyer-Kielberg. It was he who, when Mr. Christmas Møller, the former Minister of Commerce in Copenhagen, whose outspokenness had proved too much for the Germans, so that they had insisted on his expulsion not only from the Cabinet but also from Parliament, coupled with the prohibition to speak at public meetings, it was he who declared, when Mr. Møller managed to escape from Denmark with his wife and son, " it goes without saying," wrote Mr. Krøyer-Kielberg in an article in *Free Denmark*, that he " immediately became the acclaimed leader of the Movement." Every position within the Free Danish Movement was offered to him, but before accepting any post he preferred to make himself acquainted with the conditions over here. Subsequently Krøyer-Kielberg became President of the Association of the Free Danes in Great Britain and Northern Ireland, while Møller was elected to the new post of Chairman of the Council and Chairman of the Executive Committee; he is in charge of the policy and the daily conduct of the Council's affairs. One of the most valuable results of Mr. Møller's arrival in this country has been the report which he was able to give of the true position in Denmark, and that it was authentic we may be sure, not merely on account of the office which Mr. Møller had held but owing to his powers of observation. He subsequently travelled to the United States and Canada, where there are so many Danes and people of Danish extraction.

The above-mentioned monthly paper *Free Denmark* was started some time after the weekly Danish edition—*Frit*

Danmark—through which it has been possible to get in touch with Danes all over the world. Both these papers have been edited by the well-known journalist Mr. Emil Blytgen-Petersen, who at the time of the invasion was the London editor of one of the Copenhagen papers. Those of us who were brought into contact with these highly interesting and voluminous journals of the days of peace must grieve that they are now under the German jackboot. There is indeed something rotten in the state of Denmark; and when the " guests " or " tourists," as the people call them, have been flung out they will no longer have to rely for the truth on the radio from the free countries and their own underground and very courageous Press. The first number of one of these underground papers, which also has the name *Frit Danmark*, described the men behind it as people who up to the time of the invasion had differed widely in their political views, but who had sunk their peace-time differences in order to give their countrymen information of what was going on in occupied Denmark and to express the feelings of 98 per cent. of the population. " We cannot simply leave the Allies," said another article in *Frit Danmark*, " to carry the burden of the struggle against a ruthless and barbaric foe, without doing something ourselves to help. You must join in this fight. . . . We shall tell you the ways and means." Two other noteworthy illegal newspapers are *Land og Folk* (Land and People) and *De Frie Danske*. The latter gives a list of names of Danish people who co-operate in any way with the Germans, either personally or in business. Copies of this " Rogues' Who's Who " are sent to the families and employers of the people concerned. Besides the regular illegal newspapers, pamphlets and broadsheets are making their appearance in ever-increasing numbers. So far the Germans have failed to run a single one of these publications to earth.

* * *

It was obvious that, coming from such a country as Denmark, there would have been grave discontent among the women if they had not been allowed to do their utmost in the common cause. Thus it has come about that a considerable number of them are now serving with the A.T.S. and kindred organizations.

THEIR WOMEN AND THE RED CROSS

And among the beneficent acts of the Danish Council was their offer to the British Red Cross of a recreation pavilion to be built in connection with Sir Harold Gillies's hospital at Basingstoke, as a token of gratitude for the excellent treatment accorded to Danish mariners in 1923–27, after an explosion in a Danish warship which caused many casualties. This pavilion was opened in July 1942.

* * *

We must now turn our eyes to the future, the future for Denmark. That the Danes will be ready to grasp it we will realize on being reminded by Mr. Møller of the fight put up by the 115,000 citizens of North Slesvig for their liberty, a struggle which lasted from the German attack in 1864 until 1920. The Danish people have not been broken and will continue to resist the oppressor.

DENMARK'S FUTURE—AS A WOMAN SAW IT

Many of our statesmen, economists, military strategists and other publicists have considered what kind of a world this will be after the state of war is officially concluded. George Eliot used to say that prophecy is the most gratuitous of follies. But, on the other hand, if we make no preparations for the world that is to come we shall certainly be still more foolish. And, passing over those who have merely demanded the obvious rectification of the Slesvig frontier, we have at least two authorities on Denmark who have gone wider afield. The Danish lady spoke with assurance; the Polish writer will, I hope, convince everyone.

For all I know about Jomfru Fanny I am indebted to Mr. Rodney Gallop, one of our most versatile diplomats, who was as much superior to his opponents on the hockey field at Belgrade as he is to the Devil himself, for Mr.

Gallop, unlike the Devil, as we are led to believe, has been able to acquire the Basque language. And, with regard to Jomfru Fanny, he says that even her origin is a romantic mystery. In the little Danish town of Aabenraa in South Jutland, German from 1864 to 1920, there stopped, late one September evening in 1805, a stage-coach. Out of it was carried a newborn baby who was registered in the parish under the name of Franziska Carolina Elise Enger, illegitimate child of Christine Heise (the father's name being given as that of a German forester named Enger).

Strange stories were whispered about the little Fanny Enger. She had finely embroidered clothes and gold and silver trinkets engraved with a crown. While she was still only a child the woman who passed as her mother fell ill and, thinking she was about to die, told Fanny to unlock a small box of mahogany and ivory which had often aroused the child's curiosity. At her orders Fanny took a candle and burnt the letters which the box contained. When they had been reduced to ashes her " mother " said to Fanny : " Those documents contained explanations about your origin, but it would have been no help to you to know who you are."

Up to her death on 27th March, 1881, Fanny maintained that she was of royal lineage, and historical research appears to confirm that this was indeed the case. There is every reason to believe that she was the love-child of Prince Christian Frederick, who, as King Christian VIII, ruled Denmark from 1839 to 1848, and of Princess Charlotte Frederikke of Mecklemburg Schwerin. The Prince was twenty and the Princess eighteen when they met in September 1804 and fell passionately in love with each other. In December 1805 they were betrothed, and in June 1806 they were married, too late to give an honourable name to their firstborn. Their first legitimate child died in 1807 and the next, a boy born in 1808, became King Frederick VII of Denmark on his father's death. It can well be understood that the strict traditions of the Court made it impossible for the royal couple to avow the existence of a girl-child who, by Danish law, would have taken precedence of the male heir. A sad history was the Princess Charlotte's. In later years her stormy love-affair with a French music-master named Edouard du Puy caused a great scandal at Court; in 1830 she went to Rome, embraced Catholicism and died in 1840, just after her husband had assumed the throne.

Stranger and even more romantic than the story of Fanny's royal birth is that of her amazing gift of prophecy. It may be traced back to the year 1825 when, at the age of twenty, she underwent a very serious illness. No portrait of her survives, but a contemporary description enables us to see her as clearly as in a faded daguerreotype of a century ago. " She was a delicate little person with fine, regular features and a fresh complexion; her smooth, dark hair was parted in the middle, with a lock over her forehead."

Public attention was first attracted to her by her astonishing forecast of the Three Years War of 1848–50, in which the German elements in the Duchy of Slesvig-Holsten attempted to secure the detachment of the Duchy from the Danish crown and its incorporation in the North German Confederation. All the changing fortunes of the war were forecast by Jomfru Fanny, some of them twelve years beforehand. Not unnaturally her pronouncements earned her the dislike of those whose ultimate defeat she so accurately foreshadowed. She even prophesied that she herself would be placed under arrest, as indeed she was by the Germans, who took her divinations ill. To the German Mayor of Aabenraa and the enemy General before whom she was brought she announced that if they would accompany her she would show them the very spot where the Germans would be defeated and indicate the villages that would be destroyed by fire. On a later occasion the Mayor threatened her with expulsion from the town. " You will be driven out of the town before I am," said Jomfru Fanny. And this, too, came to pass when the Danes were victorious.

In the following years, however, Jomfru Fanny lost her popularity with her compatriots, for she began to prophesy the fate which was to overtake them in 1864.

"The Prussians will come and take everything," she said, "and Slesvig will groan under a harsh régime." And this, too, came to pass.

But before Fanny died she had consoled the Danes of Slesvig and regained their confidence with her vision of their ultimate redemption. They would be handed back to Denmark, she told them, after a great war in which Denmark would have no part. There would be a great sea battle in the North Sea, she added, and the water would run red with blood. The Danish troops would march into Aabenraa gay with peonies and fresh spring green, but this would not be in her lifetime.

As for the present war, we may cull some details from a little biography of the seeress written by Marie Thomsen and published at Haderslev in 1938, which the Germans have banned since the occupation. In many of her pronouncements Fanny alluded to a time when coffee and rice would be unobtainable and when everything would be so dear that little could be bought with money. In 1870 she declared that after the reunion of South Jutland with Denmark there would come yet another and much greater war in which "one would have to be for or against." Denmark, she said, would be drawn into the war and would have to look after herself. England would have enough to do to protect herself. After the war Denmark would extend far to the south and the Danish king would tether his horse at Birnbaum in Mecklemburg. "But we don't want all that," objected her hearers. "We shall not be asked," replied Fanny. "Germany will have to pay, and since she will have no money she will have to pay in land." Just north of Aabenraa there would be a terrible battle in which pardon would be neither sought nor given. On the one hand would stand the Danes, old men and boys, a disorderly army, but God would give them the victory. That would be the end, for "here at Aabenraa (in 1848) it had begun, and here it would finish."

On September 1st, 1934, a modest inscription was placed on the house where Jomfru Fanny lived and died. It is unlikely that the Germans have allowed it to remain—as if by such inept, despairing measures they could stop the wheels of destiny from rolling on.

THE VIEWS OF A BALKAN EXPERT

Whatever may be our opinion about the wisdom of Danish rule extended down to Mecklemburg, it is agreed— even by millions of Germans—that the solitary hope for the world after this war will be founded on the impossibility of further German aggression. Every attempt to stabilize the peace of Europe in the last seventy-five years has, in effect, been an attempt to prevent such aggression. " It is quite conceivable," wrote Lord Cromer in 1916, " that a peace may be patched up which may have some specious appearance of being favourable to the Allies, but which would at the same time virtually concede to the Germans all they require, in order, after time had been allowed for recuperation, to renew, with increased hope of success, their attempts to shatter modern civilization and to secure the domination of the world."

As a matter of fact, in spite of the defeat of the Hohenzollern Reich in 1918, the Baltic remained a German inland sea. Versailles reduced the German navy so that it could not compete with the navies of the Western Powers on the high seas, but it left it strong enough to make the Danish Straits inaccessible and to rule the Baltic. The annexation of Slesvig-Holsten in 1866 had eliminated the chance of that province being used by an enemy for an attack against Germany, it gave Bismarck full military control over Denmark and the Danish Straits, while the Kiel Canal, as Moltke said, doubled the strength of the German fleet by enabling it, unseen and unmolested by the enemy, to pass into the North Sea or the Baltic. By her control of the Baltic Germany has been able to separate Western from Eastern Europe. Strategically this is of far-reaching importance, for industrialized Western Europe is an arsenal of any anti-German coalition, while Eastern Europe is a reservoir of man-power and raw materials. (When considering Britain's interests in the Baltic route for communication with Central Europe, we must also mention the importance which these have for British post-war economy. It may well be that the rapid industrialization of certain Dominions and colonies will reduce to a large extent the number of traditional export markets of Great Britain; and the opportunities afforded by Central Europe must not be underestimated. This chiefly concerns Czechoslovakia and Poland, for whom the Baltic route is the only direct communication with Western Europe; their imports, with those of Hungary, Roumania and Yugoslavia, in 1937 amounted to 610 million gold dollars, while the whole import of India was only 263 millions, of South Africa 313, Australia 296, New Zealand 130 and Egypt 111. As the bulk of the goods imported by Central Europe were of German origin, their replacement by British products will have not merely an economic advantage for Great Britain, but will also help the interested countries to stabilize their political independence by checking German infiltration and consequent influence. It therefore seems very desirable that Czechoslovakia and Poland should share with Britain the active defence of the Baltic route, by providing for this purpose the necessary land forces to man the military bases along the German coast, which would permit Britain to concentrate on the naval and air protection of that area.) This defence of the North Sea–Baltic route is essential, for that is the only way of ensuring that Germany will in the future remain in a state of naval disarmament. Mr. Rowmund Pilsudski, a Polish expert on Baltic affairs, has very lucidly expounded the whole subject in his booklet *The Baltic, Britain and Peace* (London, 1942). He points out that Germany will not only have to surrender Bismarck's loot of Slesvig-Holsten, but islands in the Baltic and North Sea, in which areas military bases will have to be created to control the German ports and protect Denmark and Scandinavia against invasion, as well as to give effective naval and air support to the convoys in the Danish Straits and the Baltic.

But German islands will not suffice to organize such a defence system. It must also include some strategic points in Denmark and her harbours must be made available for the use of the fleets protecting the Baltic route. The geopolitical similarity between Egypt, the Republic of Panama and Denmark is obvious. The Allied Powers cannot allow these canals to fall under enemy influence; and there are reasons to believe that Denmark, after the experiences of the present war, will realize that the Powers concerned cannot allow Germany, because of Denmark's weakness, to control Straits which are so important to the security of Europe. Denmark should, therefore, not oppose the defence of that region passing into the hands of Powers capable of maintaining it; she should grant them the necessary rights in her territory, as Egypt and Panama have granted them to Great Britain and the United States. In exchange for this, besides a guarantee of her own security, Denmark should be given back Slesvig-Holsten, with the resulting economic advantages.

The defence area of the Baltic–North Sea route must comprise two types of base: proper anti-invasion bases situated along the German coast and second-line bases providing aerial protection for the first line and the convoys. Slesvig-Holsten, owing to its size and position, would be the natural centre of the whole system. Use would be made of the various islands, German and Danish, in the North Sea and the Baltic. Bornholm could be an intermediary base, because its size and position make it suitable for the anti-invasion defence of Sweden and for the naval and air protection of the island of Rügen and of convoys.

CHAPTER I

I AM all in favour of the North Sea. To begin with, it is just the proper size. From Harwich to Esbjerg one crosses it in about twenty-four hours and there is no time for those disagreeable encounters of a voyage say to Buenos Aires, during which one addresses a fellow-passenger by his or her family name in the first week, by the Christian name in the second, while in the third you are no longer on speaking terms. A voyage of the other extreme, say from Dover to Calais, is so brief that one does not, as a rule, attempt to form a new acquaintance. But a sea journey of some twenty-four hours is exactly right—one need not " press," as does an anxious golfer, but can make the approach in a worthy fashion, and after you have become acquainted with a sympathetic person there will be no time for you—or him—to burrow very deep below the surface and perhaps be disillusioned.

Then there is another reason which compels me to appreciate the North Sea and acknowledge publicly this sentiment. Among my readers there may be a man who dedicates himself to studying the folk-lore of the wilder people. He could tell us of the theory of propitiation that prevails among them; for example, how some tribes in equatorial Africa refrain from speaking loudly when they criticize my lord the elephant, for fear lest he get wind of this and devastate their crops. In order that he should be filled with kindliness towards them they will chant a magic invocation, they will go through complicated steps of a traditional dance or they will make the sacrifice that pleases elephants. . . . If I were to omit the proper tribute to the sea, who knows what wrath would shake it? Up to now the North Sea has reciprocated all my compliments and on this Harwich-Esbjerg passage has been beautifully tranquil. Friends of mine, on one occasion, sailed a few days earlier and were involved in hurricanes which made them ten hours late; another friend, who says he is a poet, travelled on the last occasion two days after me from Esbjerg and was six hours late. They obviously took no steps, or not the right ones, to secure the sea's benevolence.

I found that I was walking up and down the deck with Polliter, the well-known don who is a Scandinavian expert. He was on his way to study certain archives in a Jutland castle.

Presently the colours of the sea were like a thousand Persian carpets being shown to us in swift succession. Polliter and I agreed, however, that in view of our first meal on board it would be well to take some rapid exercise, so that the stewards should not put us down as very miserable performers.

Everybody knows that it is dangerous to mix one's drinks; in Denmark or a Danish boat one may do this with some impunity, so long as the potations are alternate: acquavit and then a tumbler of good Danish lager, acquavit, then lager. That is the native method, which, no doubt, has the experience of centuries behind it.

I was careful not to take two acquavits unseparated by a lager, though the brilliant, white acquavit will sing with such bravura as it dances down your throat that one would like the song to have a few more verses. But between those carefree verses a cool pause of lager has to intervene. So long as we observe this regulation we do not come to the faintest harm. What ampler proof of my sobriety is needed than the fact that after dinner I could there and then produce a list, with no one helping me, of many of the miscellaneous items I had eaten.

As it happened the one empty chair I saw was at the captain's left. No, it was not reserved, he said, for anyone. Even as Mark Antony at Cleopatra's tent, the captain had not come to talk. He was rather commonplace of aspect, while I think that his prevailing mood would verge on mournfulness. However, nearly always when a dish was placed before him he exhibited some interest, which was a compliment to the chief cook's repertory and inventiveness.

And if the mournful captain's interest could be awakened, how much more could mine? The cook in my case was a guide into a country where I had not been for years. All the table was encumbered—I should say bejewelled—with cold viands, charmingly displayed. And now and then a steward would approach with further dishes, hot and cold. We had a yellow pea soup served with bacon; we had roast duck with red cabbage; we had herrings with a yoke of egg upon them; we had herring salad duly made with apple in it; we had marinated herring; we had lobster, crab and salmon done in various ways; we had some beef, a scraped raw fillet, strewn with Russian caviar; we had caviar with oysters on toast and we had grilled mussels with a curry mayonnaise. There was brawn with creamed potatoes and beetroot; there was pickled goose with vegetables; there was goose-liver on toast (I would have been prepared to dine off that and caviar); we had fried forcemeat cakes with meat jelly and cucumber salad; we had grilled lamb's liver with mushrooms and truffles, steamed in Madeira; we had beef marrow on toasted rye bread; we had bacon, cream cheese and fried egg on toast; we had a few varieties of cheese, including one called Christian the Ninth and a green Kranterkase and a genuine Swiss and a Danish-Swiss and an almost melting Camembert on toasted white bread and an Old Holstener with duck dripping. Then we had some Danish sweets, beginning with the goodly Citron Fromage.

Reader, it is possible that when you make this voyage you will be regaled on other food. Denmark has no frowning Alps—indeed, I have been told by someone that when he was taken to a place in Jutland and informed that he was on the highest Danish hill he was surprised to hear that he was on a hill. Denmark is devoid of rivers, great or small. God was a little sleepy when He made this land, but in the sleep were some delightful dreams. There may be persons who will charge the countryside of Denmark with monotony, in spite of all the coloured beech-woods and the fjords, the laughing little brothers of the fjords of Norway, and the variegated multitude of islands and the whispering dunes. But there is no monotony in Denmark's food. Those lamentable people who are not impressed by any food, who on account of their pre-occupations or asceticism merely eat to live and thus are in a lower class than the majority of beasts, they would be well advised to keep away from Denmark.

The pleasant isle of Fanö lay in front of us, protecting Esbjerg from the sea. Our passengers were lining up to disembark, ropes and tarpaulins had been taken from the motor-cars, their owners with affectionate expressions had gone down into the bows in order to attend to them, and soon this voyage would be finished.

It was then I met Knut Petersen, white-haired and with an interesting, mobile face, so that at first I put him down to be an actor. While the ship was being manœuvred to the quay he said that we would have two hours to spend in Esbjerg before the departure of the Diesel train for Copenhagen—the ship did not always arrive so early—and would I care to have a stroll with him in Esbjerg?

A sister-ship of ours was on the point of leaving. Boxes of light wood, some twenty feet long, were now being put on board.

"Perhaps," said Petersen, "you do not know what is in them. They are full of eggs, some of them, no doubt, from my firm. I am an importer of Danish produce—eggs, butter, bacon. But now I am going to an island."

The gangways had been hooked on to our vessel. And we started, Petersen and I, to follow the other passengers.

"I daresay," remarked Polliter, who was just behind us, "that every one of those eggs is marked. I can remember reading that the system in your country is extremely thorough, and if eggs are addled it is known what farmer is responsible."

"That would be nothing," cried Petersen. "We make each hen responsible. She lays an egg, it falls into a soft receptacle and there receives a special imprint—every hen has got her own—and only after that will the machinery lift up a door through which the hen walks out to have some exercise."

"I suppose," said Polliter, "that there is nothing about hens that your people do not know. And it is a fact, is it not, that if you scatter their food all over a field, so that while they are searching for it they are continually walking up and down, they repay you by laying fine, large eggs? Ah, there is the car that has come to take me. Good-bye. I hope we'll meet somewhere again."

Petersen was looking very thoughtful. "I do not maintain," he said, "that large eggs are better, that they have more nourishment in them than small ones. But there are many folk who feel that if you happen to be the native of a small country you will be a much more cheerful and contented person than one who belongs to a world-wide empire. For example, they insist that the Danes must have the sense of brotherhood developed far more highly, that as there are few of us we cling to one another."

We had now landed and were proceeding to the customhouse.

"Was it not Sancho Panza," Petersen was saying, "who remarked that every man is what God made him and some a great deal worse? I am delighted that we love and hate each other, just as you do. There are Danes of every sort, good, bad, indifferent. And if we are expected to abandon all the usual idiosyncrasies of man when we are dealing with a fellow-Dane, what sort of people would we be?"

"It seems to me," said Polliter, who found himself once more beside us—"it seems to me that you are human beings."

"Thank you very much," said Petersen. "You put it well. The subject moved me so profoundly that I was afraid I would be incoherent. We have very strong, I could say violent, opinions with regard to one another. Some of these opinions may be utterly misguided, but they show at least that we are virile. You have heard perhaps of the Internal Mission?"

"Is it one of the activities," I asked him, "of the Church?"

Two grizzled fishermen were rolling past us and the merchant made a sign that we should hold this conversation up till they be out of hearing. After we had done so he explained that very likely they belonged to the Internal Mission and he did not wish to hurt their feelings.

"Will you not," said Polliter—he asked the question in the mildest manner—"will you not be hurting your virility?"

"Oh, well, well——" said Petersen. Then he told us how in Jutland a lay preacher of the Mission told his flock that there had been a German poet, Goethe, much addicted to wine, women and song, and that the last words of this evil man were "Light! More light!" The preacher assured his congregation that this had immediately come to pass, because Goethe descended into the flames of Hell. When he was asked if he had read anything by this man, "Not a word!" he answered proudly, "not a word!"

Polliter enquired of our informant why he thought that those two fishermen belonged to the Internal Mission.

"It is the party in our Church," he said, "which has the biggest following. It flourishes especially among those people, fisherfolk or peasants, who are faced with a hard lot."

By this time we had finished with the custom-house and Polliter had definitely left us. Petersen and I were strolling round the harbour of what had been, not so long ago, a fishing village. But Knut Petersen was obviously a merchant in a thousand, for he took the cranes, the splendid elevators, the capacious docks, the wide streets and the rows of lofty red-brick houses all for granted; he discoursed upon the other kinds of Lutherans in Denmark, those of the High Church, which is the central body, and those who are the followers of Bishop Gruntvig. That very remarkable man, I learned, was born in 1783 and died in 1872; he founded the so-called "Smiling Christendom." In his opinion the Danish Court was too much given to austerity.

"It is appropriate," said Petersen, "that the west front of the Gruntvig Memorial church in Copenhagen—of course you must go to see it—should resemble an organ, while the entire structure, outside and inside, is of pale yellow brick that produces an effect most airy and happy. By the way, Gruntvig held that a country is happy where few have too much and few have too little. His jovial face, encircled with white whiskers, gave him in his old age the appearance of a retired mariner. He was one of Denmark's greatest poets; a hymn of his composition was sung at Stockholm in the course of the wedding ceremony of the Danish Crown Prince to Princess Ingrid, and the Swedes were full of admiration. The bishop himself was married three times, in 1818, 1851 and 1854, his third wife, like his mother, being a member of the old Danish aristocracy.

"Is there," I asked, "a great deal of bitterness between the Internal Mission and the Gruntvigians?"

"Not long ago," said Petersen, "a Gruntvigian clergyman, who had officiated at a wedding, took part in the subsequent dance; certain members of the Internal Mission declared that such behaviour could only be excused on the ground that he was drunk. This view was loudly put forward by a cobbler, and when the clergyman took legal action his critic was fined. But Denmark is a country where freedom prevails, and although the people of the Internal Mission may disapprove of the Gruntvigians they are always ready to have alternate services with them in the church if there is only one building. And the Gruntvigians, if the church belongs to them, are just as hospitable. Of course in a large town each Movement has its own churches, so that the fulminations of the Internal Mission will never be heard in the Gruntvig Memorial church. But," the modest Petersen concluded, "you should have been told all this by some good theologian, not an egg and butter merchant."

I protested that my time at Esbjerg had been very profitably spent. And, as an example that one does not need to be a theologian, I recalled the satisfactory curriculum of a Sunday-school teacher who had only one lesson to impart. Every week she took her pupils out of Egypt and conducted them across the Red Sea, after which they wandered out for years into the wilderness and then they safely crossed the river Jordan. Finally they came to Jericho, surrounded by tremendous walls; a trumpet blew, the walls fell down and there the lesson ended. They were always hoping that on the next Sunday she would lead them through the town and show them all its wonders, but invariably she began again in Egypt, and the journey finished with the crumbling of the walls of Jericho."

"No doubt," said Petersen, "it was a different journey every week. And, after all, the road is less important than the traveller."

I reminded him of the philosopher who pitied anyone who for a month could sleep with the same woman and believe it was the same one every night.

Up at the station we admired the so-called lightning train, stream-lined and with a Diesel engine, that would whirl us very soon to Copenhagen. By another platform stood a local train; the venerable locomotive had, around the funnel, a broad band of red and white, the Danish colours. This old engine had been probably 10,000 miles before the Diesel had appeared and now, one thought, it had been decorated so that——

I was not sure why, and my companion, seeing that I was attracted by the coloured band, informed me that it would remain there even when the locomotive went into its shed. "That would seem strange," he said, "to you."

"But not to everyone," I said, "in England. Charles Lamb's comment obviously would have been:

> "Hey diddle, diddle, my son John
> Went to bed with his breeches on."

It was now time for us to get into the train and Petersen was asking me what plans I had. Where would I go from Copenhagen?

"Like yourself," I said, "there is an island that I want

to visit—Moen, where the cliffs, I hear, are wonderful. Which is the island you are going to?"

"A little time ago," he said, "I was ashamed. You see, I am a member of a club in England. In the town where I am living we have a nice club that meets on Thursdays and the custom is that we read papers to each other. Now and then we have a guest who does it. Some day you must——"

"Tell me, what made you ashamed of them?" I asked. He shook his head. "I was ashamed because they had proposed that I should read a paper on the beautiful Round Churches, very old they are, in Bornholm. That was all I knew about them. I was so ashamed that I am going now to Bornholm, which is in the Baltic, eight hours out from Copenhagen. You are going to an island. Why not come with me to this one? Say you will."

Our engine whistled and before the train had left the platform we were doing thirty miles an hour.

"What do you think of this?" cried Petersen. "Oh, splendid, splendid! And I see from your expression you are going with me on to Bornholm. That is splendid too."

I felt that when the builders of these trains had got a little more experience they would produce one in which we would find it possible to read. Luckily for passengers from other lands, there was the scenery, those undulating, fecund fields of Jutland. What is so exciting as one penetrates into a foreign land is to observe that there the cows behave as we have seen them do at home and there the branches of the high trees tremble in the wind.

Darkness was descending as we ran across the formidable bridge from Jutland on to Fyn. We did not even stop at Odense, the leading town of Fyn, the capital, as all good people know, of fairyland. A woman who had spoken to me on the North Sea leaned across and said how fortunate it was that there had been preserved the letter written by the callow youth Hans Andersen with reference to the publication of his earliest book. All that he wanted for his fee was twenty copies of the little pamphlet.

This was the same woman who, to illustrate how one can be non-nautical, told me a tale I will repeat, though, dealing as it does with wine, it is no vintage tale. There was the captain on the bridge who shouted " Port ! " " Port " cried an eager mate, a hearty boatswain echoed him and then a seaman could be heard exclaiming dutifully " Port ! ", a passenger believed that he was now expected to chime in. " For me," he said, " it's sherry."

From Fyn to Zealand all the train and several others and two lines of motor-cars were put on to the ferry which they told us is the largest ferry in the world. The dining-rooms and smoking-rooms, the lounges and the promenades and so forth on the upper deck are very spacious. One is sorry, after lingering about them for an hour or so, to have to sit once more in the comparatively cramped compartment of the train.

Petersen was anxious to arrive in Bornholm, which did not persuade him to regard the numerous amenities of Copenhagen with a jaundiced eye; the truth is that he scarcely looked at them. He made no comment on the reels of sewing-thread, both white and black, with which our rooms were furnished, nor did he remark upon the cardboard labels that we were invited to suspend outside the doors in case we did not wish that anyone should call us and no matter how long we might sleep.

Of course we made our pilgrimage up to the Gruntvig church, which has been placed upon a hill that rears itself a little higher than a hundred feet, so that the church is visible from out at sea. But when on the next night we set sail for Bornholm we were gazing at the myriad lamps of Copenhagen that employed the houses of the good and evil to construct a radiant house of God.

CHAPTER II

WHAT disappointments wait for us in harbour-towns. As we approach them we are captivated, from afar, by buildings and by vegetation. Usually when we make a landfall we are in a mood so unexacting that the works of man and those of Nature can be commonplace and rouse our admiration.

Petersen and I resolved that we would keep entirely cool as we were drawing near to Rönne, the metropolis of Bornholm. We would not permit our blood to circulate more swiftly on account of what we saw, the masts of many sailing vessels as they jerked a little to and fro ; a formidable, ancient warehouse of red brick behind them and a tawny-coloured lighthouse of cement, which rose out of a garden, and the pyramid of houses with a church of rugged whiteness and some other steeples and among them everywhere the trees and pine-trees over all the coastland to the north and heather on the rolling sandhills to the south. We would not be seduced by these attractions and then find, on walking through the streets of Rönne, that there was no real beauty in the place. In fact we would refrain from looking any more at Rönne from the ship, we would confine ourselves to looking at a group of children drawn up on the quay where we would disembark. They were arrayed in sombre uniforms and, with a man conducting them, had started on a song, presumably a song of welcome. We were told that they were orphans.

But however strenuously we had turned away from Rönne, so as not to lay up for ourselves illusions which, upon more intimate acquaintance, we would have to cast aside, I found it difficult indeed not to be flooded by the warmest sympathy with the inhabitants of Bornholm when I listened to the story of an engineer who said that they had sent him from another town in Denmark and the reason was that there had been a railway accident. The lines of Bornholm are, he said, of narrow gauge—they go from Rönne to the little town of Nexö in the south-east of the island, with another line that branches from it and goes up to Gudhjem on the eastern coast, while there is yet another one which traverses an agricultural district, works its way through a ravine, a small ravine, of course, and has its terminus in the far north at Sandvig, an hour's journey out of Rönne.

"You do not seem to be listening to the music of the boys," said Petersen.

I placed a hand on his, to silence his reproaches. And that silence was essential, for I was endeavouring to withstand one of the most grievous limitations that we suffer from. We have two ears and I would not like to believe that we were given two of them for a mere decorative purpose, so that the design should have a balance, but that there was an original intention for us to receive and keep apart two simultaneous currents, be they words or other noises. One of them might be addressed to us, the other one might not be meant for us at all. How much less well equipped are we for the campaign of life since we allowed this faculty, like the prehensile power of our toes, to lapse.

Now this railway accident had come to pass in a most curious way. The Bornholm practice is to let a train depart from station A for station B without informing B that it has left; there is no means by which this information can be sent. The lines are single, so that you might think it is extraordinary how more accidents have not occurred. The branch to Gudhjem is immune from all collisions, for a single train goes up and down, from Gudhjem to the junction and then back to Gudhjem. On the other lines a train occasionally meets another one at certain stations; the officials know these meetings all by heart and there was not a hitch until three men, the whole staff of a station, quite forgot that it was Sunday and that there would be a train arriving which on other days did not exist. So they allowed a train to meet it in a headlong crash, with bad results for the material. An enginedriver sprained himself in jumping off and that was the most serious human damage. How enchanting that there is an island where the whole staff at a railway station can forget that it is Sunday.

By this time we were decanting the passengers and thus, behind their friends upon the quay, some loungers and some emissaries from the few hotels, those optimistic orphans sang more vigorously than ever.

We bestowed our luggage on a representative of Dam's Hotel which is not more than several minutes' distance from the harbour; and a kindly, bearded person whose acquaintance we had made alluded to the children we had left behind us. "A choir of orphans," so he said, "delights me more than one of eunuchs."

Then he told us that before the time of Gluck the major rôles of operas in Italy were all soprano and the parts of Alexander or Julius Caesar were taken by eunuchs, enormous in bulk. Everything had to be adapted to their caprices. They did their best to distract the audience's attention during another singer's aria, taking snuff, chatting to the orchestra or yawning ostentatiously. In fact they were insufferable.

While he supplied us with these details of the bad old days we went along a narrow, up-hill street and then another, which were wholly of the Middle Ages. They were paved with cobbles, while the houses, practically all of them one-storied structures, were a brilliant blue or pink or primrose-colour with great beams of dark-stained wood diagonally fixed and charming little leaded windows, out of which you would not be surprised if anybody were to look, so long as it were not a person of to-day.

"Well," I told the bearded man, "I can inform you of some other choirs which you may possibly have overlooked. It was when those humanitarian ideas were very rife in Paris at the period of the Revolution."

"And this town," said Petersen, "or most of it, was then precisely as it is to-day. How wrong we were in thinking it would disappoint us."

He allowed me to resume and tell about a play whose edifying title was *No bastards any more in France*. A father in the play would not acknowledge his poor son and so

A View of Rönne, the Island Capital, showing the Parish Church and part of the Harbour

One of Bornholm's Mediaeval Round Churches : these curious Structures served a Double Purpose, for Religious Service and as a Sanctuary in the event of a Pirate Invasion

A Stretch of the Road which runs across the Island

the boy had for his fathers all the patriots. It was a new law and the majority of Frenchmen were agreed that it was admirable, that their country was the most enlightened, that a golden age had risen for the French. The bastards should be singing from the fullness of their hearts. And as the intervals between the acts were often occupied with songs of praise to the Republic, a good manager, who was intelligent and sympathetic, printed on his programme a request that there should be one interval reserved exclusively for bastards. All the other members of the audience were invited to refrain from singing. There was on the stage a bust of the Republic and he organized a choir of bastards who advanced with ceremony and deposited a laurel-wreath upon its brow. This met with a more general approbation than the usual procedure of encircling with a laurel-wreath the author's brow.

"Had he been well inspired," observed our bearded friend, "he might have reserved another interval when silence would have been demanded of all those who were not the authors of at least one bastard. Then such authors, very conscious of the grandeur of their country, would have raised their voices."

We arrived at Dam's Hotel, a venerable house with orange-coloured walls picked out in white. Its architect had clearly done his best to build a fortress that would not look bellicose.

Mr. Lyngby, the proprietor—a tall, thin, earnest man—was in the hall. I told him we had come to make a study of those ancient churches and whatever else of interest there might be in the island.

Mr. Lyngby nodded gravely. "There is a good deal," quoth he. "Please come into my room."

We followed him into his own apartments from whose windows one looked out on to the street. The smallish dining-room served as an office too, and though it was so early in the day a thick-set woman with a resolute expression was already at her desk.

We passed into another and much larger room, the kind of room in which a leading and respected merchant of an Ibsen drama would have felt at home. Chairs, little tables, many-coloured tablecloths and carpets—everything abounded, and a bookcase, moderately high, which ran along the inner wall, was filled with books and newspapers. "All those," said Mr. Lyngby, "are at your disposal. I belong, we all belong, to a society of folk-lore of this island. If I had some leisure I would read those books they issue, every year another one. That row of unbound volumes, I will send them to you upstairs," he said. "It is appropriate that anyone from England should be interested in the story of this island. I am not an islander myself, but from another Danish province." He was standing by a cupboard which he opened and displayed a multitude of bottles. "We will drink," he said, "to Bornholm. Will you try this island acquavit? It is not really very strong."

When I had recovered, Mr. Lyngby said that I would grow accustomed to it. "In the old days on a farm," he said, "it was the custom for the servants to be given this five times a day or six. Would you like to know their programme? It began at six—at five in summer—with an acquavit and bread, at seven o'clock the so-called 'sovekall,' a herring with a kind of porridge cooked in milk or beer, then at eleven o'clock more acquavit and bread, at twelve the dinner—meat or fish with vegetables and another acquavit—at five some bread with meat or bacon on it and an acquavit, at eight cold meat and bread with milk and acquavit again. Also they could have as much beer as they wished, but as it was not good they turned away from it, except at harvest time when they were overcome with thirst. Suppose I pour for you an acquavit that I concoct myself?"

"You said just now," I pointed out, "that you considered it appropriate that English people should be interested in the story of your island. May I ask what makes you——"

"Oh," said Mr. Lyngby, "that is very simple. The first mention of this island anywhere is in a memorandum, a report made out for your King Alfred by two merchants after they had been upon a voyage of discovery in the Baltic. And, according to this old English text, the island of Burgendaland was an independent kingdom up to the tenth century with a king of its own."

As we went up the stairs Mr. Lyngby wanted us to gaze out of the window, and indeed the courtyard is particularly noble—a quaint series of arcades support a building of half-timbered black and white.

"It is only since 1868," said Mr. Lyngby, "that this house has served as an hotel. They did not have hotels in the islands in the old days. You see, when a farmer came to town he went back in the evening, and for his meals he was invited to the houses of his customers. That is why here in the capital there was not one hostelry, no restaurant. And elsewhere on the island you relied upon the merchant or the priest, who were very glad to welcome any stranger. He would bring them news of what was going on in the great world. Those who came here from Copenhagen had a sailing ship, with not much room for passengers, but still a weekly ship that came here in the middle of the nineteenth century and the Bornholmers felt that they were not neglected. But I was telling you concerning this hotel. I have made investigations and in the year 1568, exactly three hundred years before it became an hotel, it was bought by a man, Claus Clausen Kames, who seems to have been half a Dane and half a Scot. Not much is known of him, but Margaret, his wife, committed, so the story goes, a shameful action. One day she refused to give a beggar any bread, she told him that there was none in the house, although she knew that loaves were baking in the oven. When she took them out she saw that they had turned to stone."

We were impressed.

"But that is nothing. When this island rose against the Swedes," said Mr. Lyngby, "which occurred in 1658, the Mayor of Rönne was the owner of the house and here he locked up all the Swedish officers that were not killed or did not fly back to their stronghold Hammershus, which lies near Sandvig in the north. Here are the rooms that you can have. I hope I have not wearied you, so that you must lie down."

When we assured him that this was not so, he asked if we would like to see the garden, for it was not very bad. If we had viewed it from an aeroplane this garden would have seemed to us a very gorgeous rug, in such profusion were the flowers assembled, all of them—regardless of their species and their size, regardless of their age, of everything—all of them apparently had reached perfection at the same high moment.

"I am sad," quoth Mr. Lyngby, "that you were not here a week ago, for then it was a meritorious garden. Yet it is not very bad to-day."

Around the rim of it were flowery alcoves, each provided with a little table in the shadow of a tree, and there, said Mr. Lyngby, one could breakfast. That large tree with widespread branches at the bottom of the garden was, he said, the second biggest mulberry in Bornholm. Some day he would take us in his car to Svaneke, a harbour town upon the eastern coast. The trees of Svaneke had long been celebrated and her aged and prolific mulberry, held up by wooden staves and metal bracelets, was the largest in the whole of Scandinavia.

During the remainder of the day we loitered a good deal in that old town. Nearly all the picturesque, one-storied houses looked as if the children of the giants had erected them to play with and had laughed enormously as they had painted them. We had no fault to find in that our progress was extremely slow. If someone happened to be gazing at the window of a shop, then we had to step off the pavement, which could not be done without some care, because the bicyclists in Rönne are, to put it mildly, numerous. Old ladies, who in other lands would be restricted to the fireside, sit sedately in the saddle; servant-girls in their regalia go bicycling on errands; school-masters, extremely upright, travel from their homes on large, black bicycles, and the little children with great skill propel themselves on bicycles tremendously too large for them. It made one think of Holland and the picture of a street there, drawn by our beloved Karel Čapek—two of the vast swarm of bicyclists are nuns, each with a halo proper. One considerable success the Germans had when they invaded Prague, for Čapek died and of a broken heart. The dear man with his wistful smile, his broken English—" How," he one day asked me, " does Rebecca West ? "—he would have been a subtle thorn to the polluters of his country.

From the market-place of Rönne one goes for a mile or so and reaches a pavilion by the sea. But if you prefer, whatever be your sex, to take your clothes off in a hollow of the sand-dunes or in the adjacent pine-woods, you are quite at liberty to do so. And you can return to Rönne in the lumbering, red motor-bus which is the whole fleet of its company.

From somewhere to the south of Rönne it goes through the town and finishes at a small restaurant among the pine-woods not far from the bathing-place. Then back again to where it started from, performing the round journey many times a day with one sole variation, for at night it has to go down to the harbour, taking people to the mail-boat. I have heard there are three taxi-cabs in Rönne, so that if the motor-bus should ever be laid up a substitute will take its place. The citizens of Rönne would not like this to occur; they are so thoroughly accustomed to the punctual red bus. This punctuality they hold in admiration, as they know that every passenger who is a cripple or infirm or is too young to mount the bus or to descend from it unaided, all such passengers are regularly lifted in and out by that calm, hatless man who drives the bus and sells the tickets and purveys the local gossip. No one yet in Rönne has been able to explain how this good man is always up to time. They are so proud of him that I suppose that if some twenty cripples should arrive together and in consequence the bus should be delayed, then would those kindly souls with one accord put back their clocks, so that their friend the driver should not be embarrassed.

When we got to the hotel we found we were invited to the Amtmand's house for dinner. His position is analogous to that of Governor or Lord Lieutenant, and I should have mentioned that his son—a young man reading law, but anxious to become a journalist—had interviewed me, not unvividly, for one of the small local papers. Mrs. Amtmand asked us on the telephone if we would waive it that we were not yet acquainted. Would we come at six o'clock?

There are those countries where, if you are asked for six o'clock, it is well understood that this means seven or eight. And if your presence really is required at six, then you are told that it is six and *ora inglesa*, English time. But then the Danes are not that kind of people. I said that someone in the hall had slammed a door so noisily that—would she be so good as to repeat when she expected us?

"At six p.m. Oh, do you hear it striking one? That is the sort of clock you call a grandfather, but made in Bornholm. Did you know that England brought this industry, the making of those clocks, into the island?"

I knew nothing whatsoever on the subject. What could have induced that Englishman, the pioneer, to start to manufacture those large clocks in Bornholm? "Did he find," I asked, "the climate to be specially adapted to his purpose? Otherwise it seems to me that he was an eccentric. Is the industry still carried on?"

"Indeed it is," said Mrs. Amtmand. "I will tell you all about it when you come at six. We shall have several other people dining. There was once a shipwreck and a cargo of those clocks was hurled ashore, and ever since they have been made by people of this island."

It was half-way through the afternoon when we got into conversation with the resolute lady clerk. Did we believe, she asked, that people should prepare themselves for travelling in a country by reading books about it? Evidently she did not. A lady had once come, she said, to Denmark and, before she came, consulted an old book about a land of mountains, Switzerland.

"She loved the quaintness of those chronicles, she told me. For example, in a passage dealing with the avalanches that occasionally, even in the month of August, covered the St. Gothard road, it said that 'workmen are continually employed in promoting their dissolution.'"

Petersen's expressive face caused both of us to look at him. This word "dissolution" had reminded him, he said, of someone at his Thursday Club who read a paper on some fashions of the eighteenth century. If you were travelling through Calais then and died there at some inn it was unfortunate for those to whom you had devised your property, as your possessions—those, at any rate, which you had with you—were inherited, to the exclusion of all other people whatsoever, by the King of France, and he already had disposed of the contingent rights to these possessions.

"If the innkeeper himself," I said, "obtained those rights, he must have been torn this way, that way."

"With how many sleepless nights," observed the lady clerk.

Petersen agreed with her. "He must have weighed it up," he said, "whether it was more to his advantage if the traveller sleep well and pay him handsomely on the next day or if the traveller should not awaken from his sleep and then the landlord's profit would accrue to him in other ways. Well, I suppose it all depended on what terms the King of France had sold the rights of heritage. If a considerable portion had to go to the authorities, then probably the landlord settled that for him it was more lucrative to let the visitor survive."

The lady clerk indulged in laughter. "Can you not imagine a macabre scene?" she said. "A traveller at one of these old hostelries is roused by creaking in the night. He feels that it must be a ghost and, being a brave man, he sallies forth to challenge it and drive it headlong. He goes down the staircase and discovers that the noise comes from the landlord's office where that worthy is so undecided how to act that he is tramping up and down. The visitor perceives that he is very troubled and he asks if he can be of any service."

"And if that is not the client whom the landlord is considering," said Petersen, "he might be glad to have his help. A visitor who is a qualified accountant would be quite a godsend."

After this from one category of landlords we fell to discussing others and those books of Bornholm folk-lore and what not which Mr. Lyngby had been good enough to lend us. A perusal of them would provide a very pleasant hour or so.

A youthful waiter had been hovering near us; now he said that he would fetch those books. And in his absence Petersen departed, as he had some shopping to attend to, while the lady clerk had sundry duties to perform. She waited till the young man had returned and then enjoined him—Niels his name was—that he was to help me with those books.

"Of course, of course," he said. "More is needed for a dance than a pair of red shoes. What a good thing that we learn some English here at school. My mother always said that it would turn out to be useful. And she thinks"—there was a blush on his round face—" she thinks —she may be right—that they talk English up in heaven. That is why we two are members of an English Church. The neighbours used to tell my mother it was nonsense what she thought and she replied that when we meet in heaven she would have the laugh of them."

"You really have an English church," I asked, "in Rönne?"

Niels spread out his deprecating hands. "The nearest we can get," he said, "because it was begun in England by that Mr. Irving a long time ago."

How strange that there should be a branch in Rönne of the Catholic Apostolic Church. Niels gratified my curiosity to some extent and as on the next Sunday evening he would be off duty it would give him pleasure, so he said, to take us to the service. There would not be many others present, maybe six old ladies and two men; but there would be two clergymen officiating and three other functionaries.

"To provide these gentlemen's emoluments must be," I said, "a strain for such a tiny congregation."

But the money, Niels informed me, came from England. All—and it was very little—that the Church collected there had to be sent to England and from London came what was required for salaries and other purposes. But although an Irvingite in Rönne had no great financial burden to support they frequently passed on, he said, into another Church. They had so many of them in the town, some twenty different religious bodies. As three-quarters of the people were just Lutherans, which is the Church of Denmark, those remaining nineteen bodies, some of them at any rate, were very small. A gentleman who stayed in the hotel had told him once that, as a rule, the people in them might be moved by deep religious motives, but it was as likely that they wanted, each of them, to have a Church that no one else had got, they were so independent.

While he thus enlightened me he had been fingering the books on Bornholm history and folk-lore. Finally he felt his task had been accomplished and he said that we might look into the books.

I asked him to refrain, just for a moment. Had he any other proverbs or a saying? That one of the dance and the red shoes, I said, was most agreeable.

"Another proverb about shoes?" he asked.

"No, of course not. About anything you like."

"But I have got one," he protested, "about shoes, about a woman who was very shy."

"Because her shoes were large," I asked, "and she imagined everyone was looking at them?"

"Please excuse me," said the waiter, "but you are quite wrong. One man alone was looking and she was so shy that she would not take off her shoes when she got into bed with him."

This reminded me of the doctor when he discovered that there was nothing physically wrong with a servant-girl who lay in bed. For eight weeks, she explained, she had been in that house and not a cent of wages had she received. Until she had been paid she would stay where she was. "Well," said the doctor, "I've been attending these people for two years and I've not been paid either. Make room for me."

CHAPTER III

THAT evening in the Amtmand's hospitable house —impressive, though it had no second floor, since you perceived a long succession of apartments opening into one another—in that comfortable house we met, among our fellow-guests, an officer from Copenhagen, Captain Thorvald Espersen, who had come over to the island for the annual manœuvres. He was a fine figure of a man, much darker than the average Dane. He looked as if he would be quite at home within the walls of palaces or in the field, for his appearance was most satisfactory, both grave and handsome, while one saw at once that he was just as capable.

Another guest to whom these adjectives could be applied, and in addition that of opulence, was Rönne's solitary chemist. But he had a charming modesty, for when Mrs. Amtmand told us that the fashionable quarter of the town, where everybody promenaded, was in that part of the market-place outside the chemist's shop, he pointed out that near him was the best confectioner in Rönne, who constructed pastries so ætherial that if you were to throw them up into the air they probably would float.

"This admirable shop," the chemist said, " is open till eleven o'clock at night and is responsible, much more than I am, for that pavement being haunted by the fashion of our town."

" It is a charming town you have," said Captain Espersen, and when he bowed to Mrs. Amtmand it was with an air of gratitude, as if she had designed and built the place.

As for the Amtmand, courteous and clean-shaven and imposing, it was clear that they had not appointed him to Bornholm for those attributes alone, since he possessed in a quite eminent degree the art of entertaining. Many are the hosts who toil unflaggingly, so that it may be said they have succeeded ; there are others who enjoy themselves so much that they succeed.

The bottles yielded up their contents and I overheard the

chemist saying that, two hundred years ago, there was on almost every farm an apparatus for distilling spirits, even on a farm owned by a clergyman.

"But why go back two hundred years?" the Amtmand said. "I landed once on Samsö, that small island with her twenty people. They do not feel so remote because a ship can come from Aarhus in an hour or so, and sometimes all the sea between the coast of Jutland and the little island has been frozen and the people walked across."

"But when the sea is rough," said Captain Espersen, "the crossing will be, I suppose, quite nasty?"

"Quite so," said the Amtmand, "and the Samsö population would not care to go on iron rations with regard to acquavit. So they distill their own. It is the clergyman who sees to this. I do not have to tell you that he is punctilious in the payment of the excise duty."

"That reminds me," said the chemist to my friend Knut Petersen, "for I am told that you have come to study the Round Churches; you may like to have an ancient Bornholm poem on a priest. It was written down by someone in the nineteenth century:

> Says the farmer, "The priest is coming."
> "Then open the door," says the farmer's wife.
>
> "What shall he have today?" says the farmer.
> "Rice pudding and meat," says the farmer's wife.
>
> "And what have you got for me?" says the farmer.
> "Dry bread and sour milk," says the farmer's wife.
>
> "What will he be doing all day?" says the farmer.
> "Preaching to me," says the farmer's wife.
>
> "Where shall I go today?" says the farmer.
> "Herding the cows," says the farmer's wife.
>
> "Where shall I be tonight?" says the farmer.
> "Asleep with the pigs," says the farmer's wife.
>
> "And if a louse on the pigs should bite me?"
> "Then bite the louse," said the farmer's wife.

"I am much obliged to you," said Petersen. "That is a poem I will not forget."

For some time after this the conversation occupied itself with less momentous matters. Then they were again discussing acquavit. Some regretted the old days when men were men. For example, if anybody was hurt at Farmer Hansen's house in Vestemarie there was always one good remedy which they applied—a wad of chewing tobacco dipped in acquavit.

"And boys were boys," said someone else. "We made four kinds of acquavit, and if the most inferior kind was given to a boy on his black bread when he had been confirmed—well, he was angry."

"In those days," said the chemist, "they had less butter and the children would be given bread with acquavit upon it."

"At any rate," said an elderly man, "each boy had his own. Now with sugar it was different. They fastened a lump of it on to a string and as it went from mouth to mouth each person sucked it."

When at last we all arose and bade the Amtmand and his wife farewell they came to the front door and there they showed us an array of bicycles in a large, wooden stand. Petersen and I, they said, should borrow two of them to take us out on our projected expedition to whichever of the seven Round Churches we would like to see.

And as we pushed the bicycles along the cobblestones to our hotel, we were accompanied by Captain Espersen. If we would stay here for a week or so, he said, the acting head of all the Danish army, a lieutenant-general——

"There is no full general?" I enquired.

"We possess one general, the King," said Espersen. "As I was saying, the lieutenant-general will arrive and he will stay in Bornholm for two days, I think. His car, a gorgeous limousine, will be transported with him on the ship and when he goes to dinner with the Amtmand he will make the journey of two hundred yards from Dam's Hotel with everything just as it should be, with his aide-de-camp beside him and his orderly beside the chauffeur. An official red-white standard will be fixed upon the car, while from the horn will issue that flamboyant fanfare of high notes which is restricted to lieutenant-generals. Every other car will give him right of way."

"From what I have noticed of the traffic here," said Petersen, "it seems unlikely that he will meet anything at all."

"And I can tell you," said the Captain, "that he is an unassuming man who would prefer to walk."

* * *

Next afternoon we rode to one of those old churches. The pastor and his wife and two young daughters were at home and busy in the garden. They started to apologize because we found them all, especially the pastor, in their garden clothes. And what a garden they had made of it!

The mother—a frail, anxious woman—told us that when they arrived from the United States, where they had been for many years, so that it was the native country of their children——

"Do you think," the pastor asked, "that you will go to Christiansö, a little island over there?" He waved a rather grimy hand. "Ah, yes," he said when he observed it, "let me wash before we go into the church."

As if it was suddenly wound up, his square-built figure jerked away towards the house, but the most noticeable things about him were the fierce and bushy eyebrows.

"We have got our eldest daughter married on that island," said the wife. "Give her our love if you sail over. She is married to the clergyman and schoolmaster—I mean that is one person. What was it that I was saying? Well, the garden had a dirty pond in this part. Now you see——"

She led us to a sunken pleasure ground in which an inland sea, where the red water-lilies floated, held an archipelago of rocky islands, while the mainland, sometimes hiding underneath an ambuscade of silvery-green rushes, did not hesitate in other parts to fling a promontory out into the water and the trembling lilies. Those were not the only flowers—in between the crannies of the rocks all kinds of small adventurers, arrayed in charming and bewildering uniforms, had landed on those islets.

"I am glad that you like it," said the pastor's wife. "My husband made it all, we helped a little. Now we hope that birds will come and stay upon those islands."

At this point the pastor put in his appearance. "It might possibly appeal," he said, "to migrant birds which come to Bornholm in the winter."

"Do you think," his wife enquired, "that we might have the silkehale? They are lovely, with their silken tail that looks as if it had been painted red and yellow, with a yellow fringe."

The youngest daughter clapped her hands. "Oh, will they come?" she asked.

"You see," the mother told us, "you do not have silkehale in America. At least I never saw one."

"They might fancy that you have prepared this place for them," I said.

"Especially if they are tired," said the pastor. "Now the little islands seem a trifle small for the Spitzbergen goose, the knostegaas, which travels down in winter also. But if one of them should settle here and like it she might be so happy that—you know they very seldom lay an egg in Bornholm—she might lay an egg."

"Oh dear," exclaimed the pastor's wife, "we would be famous then, at any rate the papers would be writing of us."

"What is to prevent the knostegaas from sitting elsewhere in the garden and not upon those islands?" said the pastor. "I must think about it."

As he took us to the church he said that in America he had been here and there, because the colonies of Danish people are extremely scattered.

"From our simple churches there to this one was a change," he said. "Look at the Rune stone—we have brought it in out of the weather, but it has survived a thousand years and one can still read what is on it, that the man erected it in memory of his son, the good boy, as he calls him, who was killed abroad in battle."

We were climbing up a narrow and uneven stairway in the thickness of the wall. When the inhabitants had taken refuge in the room above they would be able for a long time to prevent their enemies from reaching them. And not alone the people would be in that upper room, but cows and goats and sheep, dragged up from outside through a large, square window that would then be boarded up.

"Hard times were those," the pastor said, "and yet the people had their compensations. Like the other parishes of Bornholm, they possessed a piece of shore. It was quite an innovation when some parishes were founded in the middle of the island—that was, I believe, in 1825—with not a scrap of shore to boast of."

He was much amused at seeing I was at a loss. Wreckage —some the act of God and some of man—might have a heavy value. Purchasers would come from far and near. Officials saw to it that everything was legally conducted. And the captain and the crew of the lost vessels would be cared for. Everyone, in fact, would be quite pleased.

"If one excepts," I ventured, "the insurance people."

"They," the pastor said, "should have complained the least of all. If no wrecks were to happen no one would insure and then those companies would vanish."

When we left the village the good pastor walked beside us for a while. He said that Bornholm was not large enough to have a bishop of its own, but that it is included in the diocese of Zealand and their bishop lives in Copenhagen.

"Shall I tell you about that one, Bishop Mynster, who was here," he said, "in 1841 and sent some letters to his wife? He slept in my house and fairly well, although it rained on to his bed. He was quite good-humoured about it, as he wrote that Bornhom was, after all, only beginning to be cultured. There was one newspaper, a weekly, published in the island, and the roads were very bad indeed. The children went to school if it pleased them. Those were days! The poor bishop found that the vicarage in Rö was full of rats, but he was rather comfortable, so he said at least in writing to his wife. The venerable priest of Rö had been bedridden for a long time and he died three weeks after the bishop had stayed with him."

We thought it strange the bishop had not asked him to resign.

" The most interesting example of that," said our friend, " was at Hasle, where the priest, one Adler, was a doctor of philosophy. He wrote a Bornholm dialect lexicon as well as a series of poems and tales about Bornholm. In 1844 he was suspended on the ground that he was weak in the head. His parishioners protested, so did he. The bishop had been favourably impressed by him, but nevertheless he was removed and given a pension. After that he lived for twenty-five years in Copenhagen doing literary work. Of course, and I daresay you will agree with me, one would find it hard to deduce from a man's literary work as to whether he was sane or not. Poor fellow! Every time I go to Hasle I think a good deal about him."

Thereupon, when he had thanked us for our visit, we cycled back to Rönne. As the scenery was pleasant more than thrilling, and as Petersen was wrapped in thought, I tried to paint a scene in this old church as it would be in winter:

> Round the church a wind is crying
> And the snowflakes falling thickly,
> And the people's boots are drying
> In the warm church very quickly.
>
> To have braved the wintry weather
> Is no bad accomplishment—
> They feel very much together,
> The grim parson looks content.
>
> Awed by those great brows of blackness
> Even little boys are good,
> Nor do they fall into slackness
> In responding when they should.
>
> You behold his body swaying
> As he covers up his face,
> And you feel that he is praying
> For you and the human race.

Osterlars Church—Exterior

Osterlars Church—Interior

Rocky Coast in the north-west of the Island

The ruined Castle of Hammershus, dating from the 12th Century

> Now the wind sighs. It was harried
> From the north it loves the best,
> In its heart old songs are carried
> And the wild birds have their nest.

Petersen informed me that he had resolved to visit all the seven Round Churches. And at the same time he would like to know what else the island held of interest. Would it not therefore be advisable that we should separate and then join up again, exchanging what we had discovered? We could keep in touch by telephone. The north and east part of the island would be less advanced than Rönne, but it would not be for me as in the days of Bishop Mynster.

As he said this we were going by a barber's shop in Rönne's main street. I remembered what we had been told, that once there was a solitary barber for the whole of Bornholm and in any case it would be safer if I were to have my hair cut there and then.

It turned out that the hairdresser—a thin-faced, eager-looking man—had also lived in the United States. The spacious room in which he laboured with his two assistants was, he said, the studio; and there was so much of machinery, so lavish a display of bottles, that I felt I must congratulate the man.

"One does what is possible," he said.

When I asked him if he found it better here in Bornholm he did not say yes or no, but in the glass I saw that he was worried. Several times he hesitated and then finally he spoke. Would I consider it impossible for him, a hairdresser, to walk with me—and only up to Hasle? After I had told him I would be delighted he laughed gaily as he said that if I ever should be with a man who boasted of his travels I could win by telling how I was exactly like the gilded youth of long ago, who made the grand tour with a valet and a barber. He would be my valet and the barber up to Hasle.

Back in the hotel I saw that a big party of excursionists had come; they were from Jutland. There was music for them while they dined, and afterwards, I heard, there would be songs and speeches.

Also in the dining-room was Captain Espersen, not at the table with his brother-officers as heretofore, but with a lady. Espersen had seemed to me the kind of man who cannot tell a woman what the time is without making it appear that she, by being present, had converted it into a holy time. But now he looked extremely ill at ease. The lady, on the other hand, was very self-possessed. There was a dimple on her chin, the chin itself was formidable ; as for Captain Espersen, his attempts to smile were of the most pathetic character.

Subsequently while the railway engineer and I were waiting in the garden for our coffee we were given certain information by the waiter who provided it. As he approached us he was actively engaged in doing what we all, from time to time, if we are well-bred people, have to do, that is to make ourselves look less important than we feel we are. But he could not prevent his hand from shaking as he lifted up the coffee-pot.

" Well ? " said the engineer.

The waiter blushed a little, then he nodded at the engineer. " You see," he said to us, " in other days she was the captain's wife—they are divorced—and when she came here with those Jutlanders she found him quite by chance. Now she has told the porter to arrange it with the shipping-agents that she does not have to leave in four days with the rest of them. Who knows what will happen ? "

* * *

No one could have been more cheerful than the hair-dresser next morning, as he waited for me at his door. He was himself, he said, no weather expert, owing to the fact that he had spent his life inside a house and he had been away too long in the United States. But the Bornholmer nearly always knows, and even in the night, from where the wind is blowing. They know it partly from the breakers, so he said, if they are by the sea, and partly from the way in which the shutters creak. That is why they do not tell each other what the wind is, no more than they mention that it is not night but day. They talk of what it will be, after they have studied the horizon and the clouds. " You will be glad to hear," he said, " that for the next few days it will be fine."

As we were walking through the pine-wood near the bathing-place I asked if there was anything to shoot.

" If you had brought a gun," he said, " you might have some sport in Almindingen, the pine forest in the centre of the island. That is where the King goes—I could have obtained permission for you. Naturally there are not the animals we used to have. In the Rö district, up to the middle of the nineteenth century, we had wild horses; sometimes a stallion would be captured and made use of and then have his liberty restored to him, but now there are no more of them. As for the foxes, I have read about a fox-hunt which took place in 1799 after the service in Knud parish on Whit-Sunday. It had been announced that any-one might join who had a gun and some provisions for a day or two. But in that year the wood was green already, both the rye and wheat were rather tall, and so the foxes were most difficult to see. Six hundred people took part in the hunt, they saw no single fox and in the afternoon at three o'clock they built up fires and cooked a meal. When they had eaten it the whole six hundred of them lay down for a sleep, and then the foxes came and they consumed all that was left and later on the hunters woke and, having no more provender, they prudently went home."

We found ourselves in a delicious wood with winding sandy paths, the spears of sunlight falling through the trees, and where the path ascended there was gorse that every now and then came like a golden river overflowing its green bank; and so, mile after lovely mile, we did no more than speak a word or two.

Occasionally there would be another path that joined us and we would arrive at places where the road split into two or even three, none of them appreciably wider than the others. Bornholm deprecates the use of finger-posts and thus you often have no other guide save your intelligence. Those who rely on that, when they are in the bush or wilderness, have always, I believe, described a circle. And for those who love a whispering region, here and there a little open space, the scuttle of a rabbit and the music you can sometimes overhear, sung to each other by the woodland and the sea, what fate can be more gratifying than in such a part as this to go perpetually round and round?

Then in a clearance we came on a cabin primitively put together out of wooden and unpainted boards. Beside it was a vegetable patch and, as we got nearer, we perceived a public letter-box between the windows of the cabin. Outcrops of grey, stony earth were like so many islands in the ragged grass; one wondered at the energy which had made possible the cultivation of those vegetables. What could have induced the master of the cabin to go wilfully in search of hardship? Was he suffering from a dread disease or had a woman's conduct made of him a hermit?

Smoke was issuing in a frail column from the chimney. When we knocked upon the door a voice at once replied and asked us to step in. She—for it was a woman's voice—did not seem to be frightened or astonished. Yet a visitor's appearance could not be an everyday event.

She did not rise as we came in—her bulk made that a little inconvenient—but from her seat beside the fire she smiled at us, the smile went rippling down her chins. And with a wooden spoon unceasingly she stirred a pot; the smell which floated out of it was most alluring.

"What do you desire?" she asked and with no trace of irritation such as anchorites will show when people of the outer world invade their solitude. This amiable, obese old woman was expressing her kind nature.

We stared at one another. Some requirement simply had to be produced or we would stand there as the most unmitigated of intruders.

"What happens if one puts a letter in your box?" I asked. It is humiliating that I have to place on record such a sentence. But is there a single one of us who would not have emitted brilliant humour or deep wisdom or a happy combination of the two if he had been allowed a little time? We wake up in the night with splendid phrases—or comparatively splendid ones—that glitter in the dark. Oh, why did they delay, instead of being born some hours ago when they would have been welcomed by the company?

"Well, nothing happens to it except once a week," she said, " and then my son goes with them to the road and drops them in the motor-bus. So you can leave your letter in the box and have no more anxiety." Her smile was the sweet laying of a hand upon a fevered brow.

A silence fell upon us and the woman looked as if she had no special wish to break it.

Then the hairdresser remarked that there was somebody at Rö, a farmer, who was angry that the islanders did not restrict their speech to Bornholm dialect, which differs from good, educated Danish. "For example," said the hairdresser, " the Danish for a boy is *dreng*—in Bornholm we say *horra*; *pige* is the Danish for a girl—in Bornholm it is *pibbl*."

While he was dilating on this linguistic theme our hostess looked at him and me without impatience. There are women who would show some peevishness if strangers, unannounced, unknown to them and uninvited, were to walk into their house and then converse among themselves.

"Your son," I said, " he is not here?"

"When you live with the wolves," said she, " then you must howl. We are poor folk who earn their bread."

"Perhaps," remarked the hairdresser, " it is a letter day."

"I told you," said the woman with the slightest touch of plaintiveness, " there is no reason for anxiety. He takes them just as well as if he were a postman in a town and wore a scarlet coat. Your friend is from another country?"

When she heard that I had come from England she regarded me with interest, what time she stirred more slowly. "As to that," she said, " I do not know, but here in Bornholm humble people have it very good. Out there you will find a tree; the yellow-reddish berries have a nicely bitter taste, so that the farmers sometimes put them into sausages instead of raisins and the fruit is known as peasant raisins."

Then I told her that in England also it could come to pass for scions of the humbler classes to discover that the world is good. One of them, a Surrey chauffeur, broke into the house of friends of mine, made off with all the silver he could see and ultimately served three months in Brixton prison. There a fellow-lodger was Lord Kylsant, so that when the chauffeur gained his liberty it was considered, anyhow by some, that he had risen in the social scale. The situation he accepted was much better than his old one.

Apropos of language, as I travelled through the island I became acquainted with it, not an intimate acquaintance—but by hearing it around me, seeing it on notice-boards and on the goods displayed in shops, scanning with assistance when available those very satisfying newspapers from Copenhagen, and, moreover, living in the Danish atmosphere, I woke one day and found I could converse with Danish people in their tongue. That is not to say that I took all the hurdles in my stride—far from it; I knocked many of them down, so many that to chronicle their fall would be most tedious. For that reason you, the reader, will perceive as you go round the island with me that the conversations are recorded as if there had been no bumps, no shying at the fences, no disasters whatsoever. If the wise, old Hansard had to print the speeches made in Parliament verbatim, with the repetitions and the hesitations, with the " ers " and " ahs " not neatly trimmed away, those pages would be quite unreadable and millions of good British homes would have to make some other book their favourite literature.

We bade farewell to the fat woman and walked on and on, until a sandy tree-lined avenue went in a straight line to the scattered houses which are Hasle. You that wish to know what are the leading lions of that place will certainly be disappointed, for I do not recollect the style of architecture, if any, of the town-hall, and I know not if the harbour is commodious and safe. It is excusable, I think, that I could scarcely see the town, because as we were on the threshold of it a big dusty charabanc drove past us and a woman, that ex-wife of Captain Espersen, was in it. I had not been introduced to her the night before, yet now she half rose from her seat and shook a purple parasol at us. Some words were coming from her lips, possibly a salutation, but I could not hear them.

When the charabanc had stopped and she had spoken briefly to the driver she came up to us.

"It will not remain," she said, "in Hasle, for it is no tourist town. But I am Mrs. Consul Jensen."

"I believe," I said, as we were shaking hands, "that we are in the same hotel at Rönne."

Yes, she had seen me there, she said, and that was why she left the charabanc.

Before I had the time to thank her she was telling us the reason. She could not stay with the Jutlanders and go with them to Hammershus, because she was a little agitated, she was not as calm as one should be.

Though no one in so many words had asked the others to walk on, we were once more in motion.

Then the hairdresser was speaking. "Mrs. Consul," he addressed her, "anyone with such a head of hair, each thread of it so sensitive——"

She gazed at him, her brow was furrowed.

"Our good friend," I said, "has made a special study of the hair."

"A woman such as you," said he—there was emotion in his voice—"could never be expected to be calm."

"Yet as a rule I am," she said, "in spite of having hair like that. And you, sir, are a most observant man. I wish that others——" she was sighing.

Then we trooped into a restaurant, we ordered smörrebröd and Mrs. Consul told us why she was a little agitated. She had written to the Consul to inform him that their married life should end.

CHAPTER IV

ONE of the tawny-coloured walls of the restaurant was embellished with a reproduction of a well-known picture, that of the heroic Christian the Fourth while in the midst of a naval engagement in the year 1643. There he stands, disdaining to take cover, with his captains and subordinates about him. Such a target is he for the wicked foe that one is not surprised to hear that he was the recipient of some three and twenty wounds; but clearly they had not occurred—at any rate no major ones—up to that moment chosen by the artist, for you see the venerable monarch standing, gallant and indomitable, by the mast. " King Christian stood by the high mast "—those are the first words of a Danish anthem.

" Even if," I said, " one has not been in harmony, it is a wrench. It is a wrench for both of you. But, if I may intrude in your affairs——"

" Please do," she said.

" You have been wise in your resolve to cut the Gordian knot. Perhaps your husband is more vacillating, cannot reconcile himself to let you go——"

" I shall receive a telegram to-morrow. He will fall in with my views—he is a civilized, a cultivated man—he will present his compliments to my new husband. You may think it strange that I, who scarcely know you, should have told you all these things." And with a rueful little smile she looked into our interested faces.

" We—I feel that I can speak for both of us," I said, " we would be more than glad if we can be of any help to you. But everything seems to be going very well. Your other husband——"

" When the law," she said, " permits our marriage. There must be an interval."

" Your agitation will have settled down by then," I said.

" Who knows ? This other man, the friend you saw me with last night, he was my husband once before and he is not as civilized as one might hope. We know how to live," said Mrs. Consul, " here in Denmark. It is disillusioning if one encounters an obstructionist. What can I do ? "

As we could offer on the spot no consolation nor advice, she turned her eyes up to King Christian the Fourth, but he did not move from his mast.

" Forgive me," said the hairdresser, " but I did that myself. I left my girl and then she wanted me. Your gentleman will be the same as that."

But she continued to look troubled. " It may take too long," she said.

We murmured sympathetically, when we should have made proposals of a concrete nature. This was wretched, seeing that the woman had been altogether frank. Could we not repay her trust by telling her of a good scheme to use against the dilatory captain ?

Luckily the hairdresser was a resourceful fellow. For a while he rubbed a finger to and fro upon his lower lip and then announced that there was something one could do.

" I had intended to go back," he said, " from here to Rönne and you would have gone beside the coast to see those famous rocks and precipices. If you like, there is an inland road and we can take it. You will say ' What for ? ' "

The man was like a meadow waiting for the snowdrops, and the laughter of them you can almost hear.

" Some people say," quoth he mysteriously, " that there is no bedemand in Bornholm, that the last one died at Svaneke."

" We used to have them," Mrs. Consul said, " in Jutland."

Then the hairdresser refreshed himself with acquavit and beer, for he had something difficult to say. " My friends," he started, " when a man is born outside his time, I mean if he is born too early or too late, what can be more sad ? I know the man who would have been a splendid bedemand if they existed now. Per Strudts would be most glad to work for Mrs. Consul."

" Do you think so ? " said that lady. Then she told me that a bedemand, a praying man, was one who had the task of being the assistant of a parish priest. He and the priest would pray alternately at marriages or burials and other ceremonies. You did not have any special education to become a bedemand.

"Per Strudts," the hairdresser remarked, "has always been a blacksmith."

"I believe," she said, "they made a point of dressing in a black suit and in wearing a top-hat. And if it was a marriage he would wish them happiness, and if it was a burial he would introduce a sentence in the prayers, hoping that the next time it would be a marriage."

"Very skilfully they prayed," observed the hairdresser. "They also introduced the subject of remuneration, that they would be very pleased to have it as the people wished, in money or a cow or pigs, and that they would be glad to come and work another day. Per Strudts would have been one of the most celebrated ones if it were not that now the clergymen do everything themselves. The Psalmist talks of the despitefulness of the proud—they are too proud to have a bedemand and I am grieved."

"Well, if you really think," said Mrs. Consul, "that——"

"Of course I do! He is so grand a prayer. Naturally he is out of practice now, but if we go and ask him to become your bedemand for what you want I am as certain as one can be that he will be very, very useful."

So it came to pass that, after lunch, we turned our faces to a hilly country north-east out of Hasle. As the organizer of this expedition it was seemly that the hairdresser should take command. He strode ahead of us with a most resolute and martial air; he held himself so stiffly—yes, and even when the road ascended—that he did not need to be explicit. He desired that we should follow and not talk to him. Nor did we feel much inclination to converse among ourselves— the pace at which we were compelled to march was very strenuous.

Occasionally in this undulating, open country we could see a farmer busy with the plough and he would pay us little more attention than he dedicated to the seagulls. Only once did any ploughman interrupt his toil on our account and that was when the master of two turbulent, large dogs withdrew them from us by a peremptory shout.

At last I told the hairdresser that I had something to suggest, that we should moderate our speed, for he was killing us, and if there was no Mrs. Consul left when we had reached the bed and his prayers that the heart of Captain Espersen should melt would not be needed.

So we went at a more reasonable rate and we could talk and not be incommoded.

"I have just been thinking," said the hairdresser to Mrs. Consul—there was a sardonic undercurrent in his voice—"that you can be so happy that you live to-day."

"I am relying on you," she remarked, "to make me happier."

"If you had lived some time ago," he said, "less than a hundred years ago, you would have found it hard to be divorced."

"As if," she said, "I were not well acquainted with all that! We are no longer in the middle of the nineteenth century."

The hairdresser then turned to me, because I might not know what the conditions were. "First of all," he said, "there was a period of expiation laid down by the priest, and if the married couple after that were still as obstinate as ever in the wish to be divorced, they had to wait three years and then present themselves again before the priest, who would communicate with the authorities, and these it was who finally would make out the divorce."

But Mrs. Consul countered this. If it had been her lot to live in that abominable time, she said, then she would not have married and have put those iron shackles on herself. She would have told the Consul they must live without a marriage.

"Would he then have been a Consul?" asked the hairdresser. "I know not if his country has a rigid moral code."

"And I suppose," she said, "they do not know themselves. But he knows all about their regulations for his office. The Government of Nicaragua provided him with a small book in which they were inscribed. He has learned them carefully, so that if ever he will have to act according to those regulations he will call no shame upon himself. How often did he not, in the first year of his appointment, stand in front of me and say the regulations off by heart, what time I held the book. He was so letter-perfect in the end that there cannot have been many Consuls like him in the world. It cut me to the quick that not a single Nicaraguan appeared. But he was brave, he would not let me see how much he was discouraged."

While we had discussed these matters we had scarcely noticed that we were engaged upon a lengthy, gradual incline. But on a sudden one of us perceived, far off across the water that was underneath us to the left, a line of pallid lilac with grey edges here and there, the coast-line and the cliffs of Sweden.

Let us wait, the hairdresser exhorted us, for something else. He never once had been in that part of the island, but the bedemand had told him where he dwelt and from the summit of this road we ought to see the place.

"You understand," said Mrs. Consul, as we started on the short piece that remained, " my husband is a modest man, he——"

"You were telling us," I said, "that he would give you up without a struggle, as it is your wish, and that he would send compliments to his successor."

"He is good," quoth she. "I always said that he is good. There comes a day in every year when he and Davidsen, the wealthy merchant, of our town, assemble and observe the festival. It is the Festival of the Race, and all the Latin-Americans and the Spaniards and the Portuguese, I think, are brothers for that day. In our town, which is not a big one, Davidsen is the important man. He is the Spanish Consul and the Argentine and Brazilian, not to speak of European countries. And my husband is the only other Consul in the town."

The hairdresser said it was nice of Davidsen to let another man have Nicaragua.

"One year," said Mrs. Consul, " it is Davidsen who has

the celebration in his dining-room above the shop and then the next year—though he represents more countries and my husband only one—he comes to us. No one else may be invited, for it is the Festival of the Race, and Davidsen has pointed out that they must keep it undefiled. No one else in the town is a Latin-American or a Spaniard or a Portuguese, whereas my husband and himself are honorary ones, which is much more than to be nothing. Every year it is the task of one of them to write a paper which expounds the meaning of the day. The writer of the paper reads it to his colleague."

"Now what did I tell you?" cried the hairdresser. "That will be it, that place inside those hawthorn trees."

Upon the shoulder of a hill, not far away but separated from us by a narrow, windless valley, we discerned the tower and bell-tower of a church, all black and white. Most of the other buildings were concealed.

"Well, it will entertain you as we walk," said Mrs. Consul. We were striding at a fair pace down that hill. "A friend of mine had such a beautiful idea," she said. "It was to bring a Nicaraguan to see my husband. Naturally we could not obtain a veritable specimen, so we resolved to use a clever man, a cousin of that friend of mine, a man who was at home in Copenhagen, where he was a shipping-agent. We determined that this man should ring the bell one day and ask in broken Danish for some information as to exports that could go to Nicaragua. My husband would be gratified for all his life."

"How you can talk," remarked the hairdresser, "while we are pushing on like this. It is to be admired."

"We did not know what is the aspect of a Nicaraguan," she said. "But as my husband also was in ignorance it did not matter overmuch. The man was fortunately dark—we told him to remain unshaven for a week—and we provided him with a magnificent moustache."

The road down at the bottom of the hills was full of stones. I think that it was they which caused the hairdresser to be more critical. In his opinion, he was saying,

Mrs. Consul had to talk, for she was nervous of encountering the bedemand.

"No, no!" she said, "but I will tell you how the story ends. The Nicaraguan, that is to say the man from Copenhagen, had a great success for quite an hour. I listened in the passage. He was very, very good, enquiring eagerly about those exports, and my husband was so pleased that he invited him to stay with us for several days. The man throughout the interview had made some gestures and grimaces, throwing out his arms and so forth—I could see it through the key-hole—in the way a Nicaraguan would do. Alas, he was a little too exotic and his hand swooped down on the moustache and off it came. What could the man do then?"

The hairdresser said if it had been he, he would have run away.

"That is exactly what he did," said Mrs. Consul.

"Where there is nothing," said the hairdresser, "the King has lost his rights."

"He ran away, but the moustache he left behind and that was a great blessing, for my husband says it is undoubtedly a custom of the Nicaraguans to wear a false moustache, just as they wear false teeth in other lands. But this poor Nicaraguan, he says, was frightened that their local ways would not be known in Europe. Therefore he decamped. And his moustache is now the relic that my husband treasures most. He keeps it in a glass case covered with a piece of purple velvet. When he wants to do a person special honour he displays it. 'You behold,' he says, 'a real, false moustache of Nicaragua. The owner gave it me, at any rate he never asked me to return it.'"

Scarcely had she finished when we reached the village of the hawthorn trees. So few in number were the houses that we did not have to ask the way to where the blacksmith dwelt. He was engaged in hammering a horseshoe; when he caught sight of the hairdresser he stopped.

The hairdresser congratulated him on being busy.

Yes, he said, he worked for all the countryside and there was always something to be done.

Meanwhile we had studied him, his lofty brow, his weather-beaten face, his eyes that were more fitting for a sailor than a blacksmith.

Then the hairdresser went with him to the dark interior of the forge, and we could see they were confabulating. As we watched them—we had nothing else to do—it seemed to us that Strudts was being obstinate and that the hairdresser was trying to persuade him.

Naturally it was Mrs. Consul who regarded them with most anxiety. And I did what I could to soothe her. I was saying that it was a happy omen that this village stood in hawthorn trees, considering that ancient Greeks would carry branches of it for the marriage ceremonial. To them it was an emblem of hope.

"Oh, thank you so much," said Mrs. Consul.

"And these hawthorns," I said, "are exceptionally fine ones. They are trees, not merely shrubs."

"I wonder what is keeping those two men?" said Mrs. Consul.

Finally they did come out, the blacksmith first, and it was evident that he had come to a decision. He compressed his lips, but they were twitching. He then spoke to all of us.

"My friend," he said, "wants me to be your bedemand and pray for you. He thinks that I have a vocation for that holy office."

"May your entrails roast in hell!" exclaimed the hairdresser. "You are the most provoking person."

He turned half round to the interrupter and with dignity he asked him not to be so wrathful.

"After I have brought these people here on purpose," said the hairdresser, "that reason you put forward, it is next to nothing."

"On the contrary," said he, "but they shall judge."

"I wish you would not listen to the fellow," said the hairdresser impetuously. He was so vehement that a plump sparrow, settled in a lower branch and feasting on a scarlet fruit, broke off and flew away when he would have preferred to bring the banquet to a logical conclusion.

"Let me tell you," said the blacksmith, "how it stands.

The pastor of this church is a good, pious man. Not once in all the time has he invited me to help him in the praying—he and I, then he, then I, as it was done in former days between me and the gentleman who was the pastor then. How can I with this other pastor start again to be a bedemand and then not be a seemly one, but praying all alone? It would be so presumptuous that both the clergyman and God would turn against me."

"Always thinking of yourself!" exclaimed the hairdresser. "God would not turn against this lady, Mrs. Consul."

With a deprecating sweep of his large, work-soiled hand the blacksmith bowed to her. "If you will pray," said he, "then God might grant you everything. My intercession would be out of order, as I have explained, and it would only do you harm. What do you think?"

She hesitated. "It is not," she said, "as if I had not tried. But one can always try again."

Then spoke the hairdresser. He said that he was going back at once, he had his business to attend to. "So goodbye," said he, "good-bye to everyone."

"Good-bye to you," the blacksmith said, apparently not bearing him the least ill-will. "In such high matters one should not be devious but very simple and quite easy to be seen through, so that God shall not be worried, have no reason to complain."

The hairdresser had gone a step or two, and now he halted and he made a comment that was not polite so much as picturesque. "Oho!" he said, "quite easy to be seen through! Was it not the devil who employed those words, that he was easy to be seen through, after he had put himself into a pair of glass trousers?"

CHAPTER V

THOSE of us whose fate it is to sojourn in the less frequented parts bring back, from time to time, a tale of lodgings so incredible that we are not believed. And which is worse—the wild conditions that we undergo or the refusal of an audience to accept them?

A good deal of the unbelief that we encounter springs out of the lurid tales we spread of what has happened in a bedroom. Occasionally it has not happened, for I daresay that a good many of my readers, when their bedroom out beyond the north-west frontier was invaded by a lovely damsel, felt uncertain of the local etiquette. She may have come for you to demonstrate how adamantine is your self-control, but on the other hand it may be otherwise. And obviously to maintain the passive attitude is foolish, since there is an even chance that this will be rebuked at breakfast and there will be added all the bitterness of self-rebuke.

One may be obliged to share a smallish room, as I once had to do at Sparta, with another man; when I retired he had not shown himself, but they informed me that he was a reputable fellow and a clerk. Now the window had a great disinclination to stay open and the door was not inclined to shut, so that I sallied forth and found two rocks, the first of which I placed upon the window-sill, the second one behind the door. And when the clerk arrived I rose and rolled that little rock against the door, the other one I fixed so that the window should not close. The clerk removed his bowler-hat, his boots with their elastic sides and swiftly fell upon his bed. I wondered in a mild way whether he was hoping to protect himself against the freshness of the air or else against the madness he assumed in me or if his preparations for the night were never of a more elaborate kind. But all was well and when I woke up in the morning he had disappeared.

That Bornholm village of the hawthorn trees does not pretend to give for man or beast more than a modicum of shelter. To be accurate it has one room, a barn in which the threshers work and which is used for other miscellaneous purposes. Thus we were told that on the 22nd of February, otherwise the " Day of Peter with the warm stone," all the neighbourhood assembles for a dance. That is the time when, as a rule, it starts to thaw, the sleighs will soon be put aside and in the old days that was when the sorry roads thrust all except your nearest neighbours from you. They demanded, therefore, one more evening of enjoyment. When the dance had finished it was customary for a number of the guests who lived a long way off to sleep upon the floor on rugs and mattresses which all the householders provided. Some of them would reappear and be spread out on subsequent occasions when a man from elsewhere on the island had to spend the night, owing to the weather or the roads or his own state.

We were taken, Mrs. Consul and myself, into that wooden room across the creaking floor and we perceived that mattresses with rugs upon them had been hospitably laid for us. The blacksmith wished us a good night and then withdrew.

" Of course," said Mrs. Consul, " there is some advantage in a room like this one, as it has no furniture to knock against. I am not sure, I am not sure——"

" But there are mattresses," I pointed out.

" Oh, it was something else," said Mrs. Consul, " that I had in mind. We Scandinavians cannot do without our symbols. Personally I should hate to spend an evening at a theatre and look on at a play which had no symbols in it. Tell me, do you think that love, the greatest love, can ever be like sailing over a calm sea, like walking through an empty room ? Or do you think—now may I sit down next to you ? " she asked. " Come, here it is, your mattress." Saying which, she pulled me by the arm and there I sat beside her.

" My dear friend," she said, " it is to me as if we had been known to one another many centuries ago. This island will be sacred for us now for evermore."

" We ought to know the story of it, should we not ? " I said. " I see you have a little guide-book with you." And I dived across her knees to pick it up.

"Another time," she said.

"How shameful it would be," said I, "to visit Hammershus, as we shall do to-morrow, and know nothing whatsoever. Here it is," I said. "It seems the south of Sweden in those days belonged to Denmark and the most important personage was not the King, but the Archbishop —Roman Catholic, of course—of Lund. Three-quarters of Bornholm was under him, all administered from the grand old castle of Hammershus. This arrangement lasted for 373 years."

"If you propose to tell me about all those years," said Mrs. Consul, "then I might as well go to sleep. Let us be quick and get to Prinzenskjold and Koefoed—they killed each other. But all that was long ago." Her hand was resting upon mine.

That interested me, I said, and I would find the passage. There it was, that Prinzenskjold, the representative of Sweden, did not deserve his tragic fate. This governor decided that no class of the community should be exempt from paying taxes, he laid hands upon the clergy's tithes, comparatively speaking they were wealthy and more sensitive than others. In the ordinary way of things this would have gratified the peasants, but as times were bad the taxes were made heavier for everyone and Prinzenskjold was, after all, the representative of Sweden which had conquered them and now was ruling them against their will, so that his virtues, even with the peasants, were obscured. He posted tax-collectors up and down the island. When the Swedes had worked all day collecting taxes and imposing generally the will of Sweden they relaxed at night by getting drunk, and one night in December 1658 the bath of blood began, with every church bell ringing. This was done so that the Swedes should not go to their death in heathen fashion, but in a true Christian manner should ride up to heaven on the music of the bells. It was ordered by the clergy, notwithstanding all the hatred which they had for Prinzenskjold and his collectors. When you are a clergyman, they said, you must behave in a religious spirit; some of them assisted personally in the ringing of the bells and with the utmost charity they pulled and pulled, no matter if their arms were aching, and out of the total of 965 Swedes in Bornholm all but twelve were put to death, most of them while they were sleeping, whether drunk or not so drunk.

It was then that the old-fashioned lamp behind us grew more dim and threatened very soon to go out altogether.

"But you are disappointed. One can hear it in your voice," said Mrs. Consul.

"I would have liked to read," I said, "about that other man you spoke of. What did Koefoed do?"

"Well, I know all about him. He is one of our heroic Danes—he organized the whole affair and when that Prinzenskjold was killed he put upon himself the sword and hat and pistols of the murdered man. So now you know what Koefoed did. I think it will be wiser if you close the book, it is too dark for you to read."

I said that after her exertions of the day, especially that walk behind the hairdresser, was she not very tired?

"Oh, not at all," she said.

Perhaps then, I suggested, she might tell me just a little more. I knew that now the Swedes and Danes are on the friendliest of terms. How long ago did that begin?

"God and the saints!" said Mrs. Consul, "you live only in the past. So let me tell you of the kindly spirit that prevailed, more frequently than not, between the islanders and the archbishops. One of them had made himself so popular that they insisted on presenting him with a superb, incomparable diamond. It lay, so said tradition, underneath a rock in Almindingen, that pine forest in the middle of the island. Hundreds of them, armed with ropes and iron bars, went off with the archbishop in their company, he on his white, official steed. They planned to roll or pull the rock aside. And when, after tremendous labour, this was done, the diamond could not be found. But there remained two other famous rocks which from of old had gathered pilgrims round them and been venerated very highly. There it was that the devoted populace were wont to dance pre-Christian, ritual measures, some of which were invocations to the Goddess of Fertility. They say—but we can talk of that another time. The faithful islanders marched off into the woods and struggled for I do not know how long before that second rock would move. A number of them strained themselves and came away with bruised and bleeding hands from a collision with a tree or with a comrade's boots or with the rock itself. But gallantly they would persist and in the end the rock was dragged away so far that one could search in the soft ground beneath it. And they could not see the diamond. What did they do?"

"One can be sure," I said, "that some of them swore horribly."

"And some," said Mrs. Consul, "took it in a different way. 'God help us all!' they cried. I should have told you, but it slipped my memory, that those three rocks were all so balanced that a child could make them oscillate, but to detach them from their site, that was a very different matter. Stones like that are known as rocking-stones and other countries have them too. Well, the good, generous people shouted that they would not rest until the third stone had been hauled away; the diamond would surely be discovered under that one. They were bent on paying the archbishop all the honour he deserved. 'But Bornholm will be mulcted of her curiosities,' he told them. 'You are more to us,' they answered, 'than the curiosities can ever be.' He was obliged to them, nay more, he was profoundly grateful; if they would refrain from interference with the last of the three rocking-stones he would regard it with the keenest satisfaction. He could tell them also that this deference to Nature, this refusal to upset what Nature had contrived, would go down very well with God. He therefore begged them to desist. He would take their kind intention for the deed. They remonstrated with him rather stubbornly, but it was done according to his will. Now it is beautifully dark."

"But how unnatural," I said, "all that dislodging was."

"Ah, yes," said Mrs. Consul, as she lay down on my mattress.

* * *

The blacksmith recommended us to make a detour, so

that on the way to Hammershus we would go through the Finnedalen valley. But before we left the farm we heard a sound of ten or fifteen children's voices glittering with laughter. They were in a room constructed of pale yellow bricks.

" That will be the school," said Mrs. Consul. " I believe that they are being told a fairy-tale of Andersen's or something of that sort."

" The only other time," I said, " when I have stood outside a school and listened was in one of the oases in the south of Tunis and the boys were being told not fairy-tales but very much the truth."

" How proper that the Facts of Life," said Mrs. Consul, " should——" Her loftiest emotions had been stirred.

I was afraid that we would interrupt the gay proceedings in the classroom. So I ventured to hold up a finger to my lips and Mrs. Consul, taking it by no means ill, subsided.

Then I whispered that the master of that school in Tunis was a Frenchman and I heard him talk of Agincourt and how the French were vanquished. " Does it not appear to you," I said, " that if a nation can produce a teacher of that kind it will always in the end remain unconquered?"

Then the schoolmistress came out upon the threshold, a benignant and matronly figure in a close-fitting blue dress, I think it was, with a white band round the neck by way of ornament and gold-rimmed spectacles that shone conspicuously from her ample, roseate face.

" Good morning," she said to us, " and you are very welcome here."

Behind her and at either side was the reception committee. Boys and girls, they nearly all had flaxen hair, and then it struck one that there was not such a difference in their ages as one would expect.

" Your school," I asked the homely woman, " is for a wide area?"

" So wide," she said, " that several of the children, four of them, sleep in the farm and go back once a week."

How came it then that, educating all the youngsters of the

region, they should all be, roughly speaking, of one age? Had there been a sudden patriotic outburst to provide the district with another generation? Had the cautious parents then been satisfied? It seemed to me that if I could collaborate in the production of such joyous creatures I would still be nursing the inviolable hope to populate the world with further specimens.

The schoolmistress and Mrs. Consul had been speaking to each other. The result was that a lad in shapeless and discoloured trousers—nearly all his colleagues favoured knickerbockers—pushed his way into the foreground with a violin.

"Your National Anthem," said the schoolmistress.

But there was no necessity for her to give this information, as I recognized the tune quite easily. What village school in England could receive a Danish visitor, arriving unannounced, with his own Anthem on a violin? Perhaps, however, that small boy in Bornholm was a prodigy, and so it will be kinder if I do not state his name, for he may not fulfil his early promise.

When the boy had played his final bar we patted him upon the head and we were wondering what we could offer him and his companions. We had some chocolate with us and we would most willingly have left those iron rations, but the whole amount was lamentably small. It is quite true that elephants do not disdain to take in buns, but that may be because they are too courteous to reject those trifles. While we hurriedly considered what, if anything, to do, the kindly schoolmistress began to speak. Would we be good enough, she said, to give the children something?

"Naturally, naturally," we assured her, "that is just what we propose to do. What would they like? After all, you know their tastes much more than we do." And we warned her of the insufficiency of chocolate.

"Children!" she exclaimed, "run in and fetch your books."

In less than half a minute they had reappeared and they were flourishing, each one of them, a paper-bound, diminutive affair of miscellaneous pale colours. Shyly they extended them, these books that were for holding autographs. As yet no entries had been made in them.

"How can I ask you"—she half shook her head—"to sign them all?"

"But that," I said, "is nothing. It is nothing in more senses than in one. If only we had come prepared . . . if in this neighbourhood you had a shop——"

The children now were flocking round us and as we inscribed our names they uttered exclamations of delight and varied this by whirling on their toes in ecstasy.

Have we not often, when about to meet a stranger, asked ourselves what they are going to meet? Those children did not meet us in our garb of every day—we were so dazzled by the sunlight of their happiness that we could do no more than lend ourselves for it to play upon, so that the loveliest of masks was given us, heart-breaking masks of youth and innocence.

"What a splendid day it is for everyone!" declared the mistress. "We will celebrate it by—by—yes, we will escort our visitors along the road. Now put yourselves all round them."

This manœuvre they accomplished swiftly and they now were in a mood from which the shyness had evaporated, an enthusiastic and hilarious mood, so that they raced and sang and danced, all simultaneously, as far as possible. We in the centre of them had, of course, to run as rapidly as they, though we could leave out the embroideries of song and dance.

Do not let me give you the impression that we sped across the land unwillingly. No, the exuberance of those delightful children had infected us; we asked for nothing better than this interlude. But afterwards, in meditation over the performance, we were very certain that our progress had not been æsthetic, and particularly when compared with that of our blithe escort. It is true that we were burdened both with years and rucksacks, but with all allowance made we must have been a sorry spectacle, as we went lumbering on our way. Not once, however, did a person of the escort laugh at us; they laughed indeed, but that was *joie de vivre*.

Then we came to where the wanton meadows took a sharp turn towards the sky. Yet this did not persuade the children to conserve their energies. They darted up that hill as if it were the fortress of an ogre lying dead with his ill-gotten gains, a quarry waiting to be captured.

" Flowers, those wild flowers ! " I gasped.

The children understood me, but their interest was not excited. I confess that those few flowers which I could see were unremarkable.

A drastic step had to be taken. So I plunged through the surrounding children, rushed a yard or two and hurled myself on to the ground. " Oh, flower, flower ! " I exclaimed. " Come here and look."

They gathered round me. Some of them were searching in the grass and enterprising little fingers tried to thrust themselves beneath me, since I might have fallen on the precious object.

When I rose I pointed to the place where I had lain and said that as the flower had seen fit to sink into the ground one must resign oneself. Let them go back to where the mistress, very sensibly, was waiting for them at the bottom of the hill, we others would continue on our journey. Then, to clinch the matter, I shook hands and thanked them warmly. So did Mrs. Consul, after which we strode away. Of course, we turned round, more than once or twice, and waved to our late escort an affectionate and grateful and a very sad farewell.

It was not only due to weariness that we walked on in such a sober fashion.

" When you flung yourself upon the ground," said Mrs. Consul, " I could not have run another centimetre. When I was a hockey-girl . . . ah, yes."

I told her that I knew how strenuous a game it is. But that did not affect our host and captain H. G. Wells when he took part in those tremendous games at Easton which he has immortalized in " Mr. Britling sees it through." Generally he himself was centre-forward and the referee, his vocal commentary in staccato, high-pitched phrases being dedicated now to one and now his other function.

"I did not realize that you know anything about the game," said Mrs. Consul.

"And no more," said I, "did many of those Easton players. They would have it that an evolution I performed, the way that I revolved, was not according to the rules; and thus there often was an outcry, which I thought unjust, before I could get really going."

Presently we came to Finnedalen, the delicious, wooded valley where the birch-trees are like soldiers leaning on their silvery lances to protect the red and purple wealth of junipers behind them. With a ridge of hills at either side of us we walked enchanted through the winding avenues of Finnedalen. Certain rumours of unpleasantness had spread abroad, the dull green of the birch leaves quivered as they told us of it, namely, that the willows, arrogant in flashing white and purple clothes, had publicly declared that one must draw the line at ash-trees on account of their excessive ugliness. So early would the leaves of them fall off and afterwards there would be nothing but a melancholy spectacle of grey and black. To this the ash-trees had replied that they were very, very useful, but this argument the willows had not deigned to notice. Then the ash-trees murmured that they were related to the lilac and the jasmine, whereupon the willows, with the narrow leaves all trembling, said they really might have mentioned that before. A reconciliation was effected there and then, and Finnedalen was a valley full of peace.

There was a meadow at the end of it and then, in front of us upon a lofty mound, the formidable ruins of the castle sat enthroned in grim serenity. There is an inscription on a granite slab to celebrate the triumph of the islanders. I am sure no islander can read it and remain unmoved. It must be quite impossible for him to roam about the purlieus of the castle and behave regrettably. You see no scraps of paper left about, no débris of a meal, and there is no unseemliness whatever. The one notice is to tell you that if you climb up on to a certain piece of the surrounding wall to see the view that probably will be your last view on this earth.

Some of the castle still survives, the dungeons which have now more ventilation than in other days, the solid storerooms where the tribute (usually geese or pigs or other produce) of the islanders was placed when those archbishops had dominion over Bornholm, the grand, old greyred keep of which the outer shell, despite the vegetation on it here and there, proclaims as it has always done that it is perfectly impregnable.

Upon a piece of granite that projected like a bastion from the castle wall there stood a lonely figure dressed in khaki. He was gazing with a rapt attention down upon the stern line of the coast, so much in contrast with the suave and sandy stretches of the neighbourhood of Rönne.

Then we saw that Captain Espersen—for it was he—became extremely moved by the magnificence of jagged rock, bay after little bay of it, the rocks and their old enemy, the sea, dyed to harmonious tints of deepest azure by some passing cloud; and then, with brilliance in the air again, the combatants arrayed themselves in sharply different colours and a most important seabird, with his livery so white against the greyness of the sea, fulfilled his duties as a herald to declare that the perpetual conflict was resumed—so stirred was Captain Espersen that he was stretching out his arms.

"Shall we go up to him?" I asked.

"He is a hard, hard man," said Mrs. Consul.

I could feel her fingers on my sleeve and she was shuddering.

CHAPTER VI

CAPTAIN ESPERSEN had come officially, he told us, to the northern end of Bornholm. And as there was not much to detain him in the small twin-towns of Allinge and Sandvig he had seized the opportunity of walking on to Hammershus, where in the bygone centuries——

" So now you are romantic," Mrs. Consul said. " And when did you begin ? "

He flushed. " I am afraid," he said, " you do not know me very well."

" You are the hardest man," said she, " whom I have ever met."

It was instructive to observe how Mrs. Consul varied in her attitude to Captain Espersen, for in the dining-room at Rönne she behaved as if she was quite sure of landing him, whereas at Hammershus her mind was filled with apprehension. As she had not in the meantime heard from Espersen or anything about him one might think her change of mood was unaccountable. But in my limited acquaintance with her I had realized that she was no believer in a life of dull monotony. I wished her well . . . perhaps indeed I might be of some little help in her campaign.

Then we proceeded down that hill upon a wide and very comfortable road, with views of a small harbour underneath us to the left and, on the other side of it, the last extremity of Bornholm.

" It was there, at Hammershus," said Espersen, " that Ulfeldt was imprisoned with his wife. But what a man ! I always knew that he was a big traitor who was Governor of Copenhagen and Chancellor of the Exchequer, who enriched himself by striking coins that were base and shamefully neglecting the defences, so that the Swedes won that easy victory of 1643. The man deserved——"

" And his poor wife," said Mrs. Consul, " that poor Leonora Christina, a natural daughter of Christian the Fourth, did he not neglect her too ? "

" Very probably," said Espersen. " The man deserved

to fall, but that was a time when the greater nobles were very independent. I have been reading up about him."

"One is glad to know," I said, "that finally he was imprisoned."

Espersen explained that this did not occur until there was a new King on the throne and, more especially, a Queen, Sophia Amalia, a Saxon princess who detested Leonora Christina on account of her beauty and her talents. Then he pointed to the pale gold of the tiny bay of Sandvig that lay spread in front of us. "As beautiful as that," he said.

Presently we came into the little town and in the queer-shaped market-place, constructed on a slope, there was a stately sort of building. Out of the main door a man emerged who was expensively attired. His gait was rather reminiscent of a turkey cock's and one could see that he did not regard himself with disapproval. Yet he had allowed his figure to run very much to seed.

This gentleman went strutting through the market-place and it was a surprise to me when he took off his hat politely to a somewhat threadbare individual.

"I see," said Mrs. Consul, "that you are astonished."

"If one were to judge them by appearances," I said, "the other man might be his servant."

"Probably he is," said Mrs. Consul. "We have got the custom here in Denmark for employers to salute their employees."

A curious, old house was our hotel—no doubt a painter would at once erect his easel in the yard which is a very picturesque and ramshackle affair, surrounded more or less by wooden balconies that look as if they cling to their position chiefly through the force of habit. Then there is the kitchen, a surprisingly large modern room that opens to the yard. Perhaps it has been newly built for the accommodation of the reigning cook, a woman who would be severely hampered in a room of average size.

The public room to which they took us had been hung with Chinese lanterns and with bundles of oats, barley, wheat, while paper flowers united them in a long, undulating garland. We were told that the young natives of the town would be assembling in the room to hold a dance.

My companions were not ready yet—this one could see —for a complete, unhesitating reconciliation. This would have to be a gradual, very gradual, process. And it would be necessary for a meeting to be brought about upon a neutral ground.

"Will you tell us something more," I said, "concerning those two prisoners of Hammershus?"

"Perhaps," said he, "you have not heard about a book by Viscount Molesworth, who was a disgruntled diplomat. He told the English public all that tragic story, not for altruistic reasons but because he was vindictive and he fancied that the Danish Government would be embarrassed."

Mrs. Consul said she had not heard of him.

"When he had lived two years in Copenhagen," said the Captain, "towards the end of the seventeenth century, he was recalled, as he had made himself obnoxious. He was arrogant, in fact you would not say that he was diplomatic, for he would persist in hunting through the King of Denmark's private game preserves. The book he wrote was to inform, he said, the world about the arbitrariness and despotism of the Danish Court. As an example of its brutal methods he described the persecution which Count Ulfeldt had to suffer."

Mrs. Consul said that she would like to know how the degraded scoundrel got away from Hammershus.

"Only," Espersen explained, "by renouncing his possessions, save for a single property which Ulfeldt had in Fyn. He thought he would be better off in Sweden and he joined the Swedish King who was at war with Denmark. Later on he joined in a conspiracy against the Swedish King and fled to Copenhagen. And his wife, whenever she could manage it she followed him, though she was handicapped by having to give birth to many children."

"Always, always it is the woman who suffers," said Mrs. Consul.

"Ulfeldt lost his life in a disaster on the Rhine; before

that happened Leonora came to England to recover twenty thousand patacoons, a sum which had been lent to Charles II by the Count when Charles was living in the Low Countries in exile."

Lovely word! Fancy saying to your servant in the morning: "Fill my purse with patacoons."

Then Espersen related how the King of England had behaved. And Charles did not excuse himself by pointing out that Leonora, through her father, was his cousin, so that everything between them was domestic, an affair in which the commentators of that time or any other time ought not, if they have respect for privacy, to meddle. He did not deny that an amount of patacoons was due to her. But she was taken down to Dover and—without the patacoons, of course—she was compelled to get on to a boat that sailed with her to Copenhagen.

"The poor woman," Mrs. Consul said, "had been a faithful, loving wife. That was her only sin. We women——"

Espersen looked rather sympathetic. "It is true," he said, "that she was very faithful, but they were not hard on her because of that alone. Owing to the Queen, she was thrust into the Blue Tower at Copenhagen and she stayed in it for two and twenty years, until the Queen was dead."

"And all the time," said Mrs. Consul, "it was Ulfeldt whom they should have punished."

"So they did," said Espersen, "according to the methods then in vogue. As he himself was not available, a wooden effigy of him was made, it was decapitated and then quartered, while the Ulfeldt palace was demolished and a sandstone pillar was erected on that ground as a memorial of his many crimes. One year after this there was that accident in which he lost his life. As for the widow, we have got her celebrated book, *The Complaint of Leonora Christina*, a book that was published about two hundred years after it was written, because the manuscript was kept in Austria in the archives of her husband's family. As a work of literature it has great value, I am told. And

I," said Espersen, " who read it not on that account, I was absorbed."

Then Mrs. Consul laid her hand so tenderly upon his knee. " What do you think," she said to me, " of this, my friend ? "

" Now, now," said Espersen, protesting mildly, " do not draw me in. It is with Leonora that we are concerned."

" You may remember," I remarked, " that Clemenceau told somebody he was at work upon a treatise and the subject of it the idea of God. The other person was astonished that the old man should be writing on a topic that was non-political. ' Oh, well,' said Clemenceau, ' I shall find out a way to shove in Poincaré—*le fourrer dedans*.' "

" The worst of it," said Espersen, " was that in prison she was rarely left without a warder, male or female, in her cell, and most of them she found obnoxious. For example, when the governor of the gaol permitted her to keep a tame rat in a parrot's cage one of the wardresses destroyed it with a lighted candle that she thrust up through the bars. Think of the kind of woman Leonora was—her gentleness, her piety—she spent a good deal of her time in writing hymns. And her embroideries, of which a number are extant, were beautifully made. When she was out of silk she had a way of using her own golden hair."

Before I went up to my room that evening I strolled a little in the yard. The kitchen door was open and the cook was in a rocking-chair. The flames made her red face more fiery still ; she mopped her brow and she exuded satisfaction.

> When all the pots and pans
> Hang shining from their pegs,
> The poor old cook is free
> To rest her weary legs.
>
> She labours all the day,
> And scarce one thought she gives
> To the fine daughter who
> In guilty splendour lives.

Christiansö, the Harbour and Town

The Bridge connecting Christiansö (in the foreground) with Frederiksö, whose Fortress Tower is seen to the right

Gudhjem, the Harbour

Helligdommen, the famous Sanctuary Cliff

> But when the dear old soul
> Sits rocking to and fro,
> She watches with a smile
> The red fire's gorgeous glow.

I do not know if she has got a daughter and those lines may have no more than what is called artistic truth. But what she had accomplished was a pudding that I shied at. A rice-pudding in its proper place is very well, but one may be reluctant to embark upon the Sandvig variation, in the midst of it a lump of butter and with powdered nutmeg sprinkled over it and then the whole concoction inundated with a glass of beer—or, if you like, the beer (in which there is no alcohol, but sugar) can be served you separately in a glass.

* * *

In the night I settled that, as Captain Espersen and Mrs. Consul were by this time on more amicable terms, I could depart. And it was very early in the morning that I left, having written them a note to say that it was urgent, that I had to meet a friend at Svaneke. It was true that Petersen had telephoned that in a week he would be there; and this would give me time to visit the small group of islands, Christiansö and Frederiksö and so on, that were visible on the horizon.

Brilliant was the sun as I set off along the coast that curved irregularly to the south. Even on the dreariest of days when the grey sea is unresponsive and there is no laughing glitter on the surface of the rocks it surely must be a poor heart which is not thrilled by that enchanted stretch of shore. The path goes winding in and out, perpetually seeking other levels; at one moment the green lizards, venturing out of their comfortable homes just at the margin of the sand, will in a single rush climb to the fairway, then for twenty feet you also have to climb; but you are lured unceasingly from one small bay on to the higher ground that separates it from the next one. When it has been raining and the sky is washed into the suavest memory of sapphire, when the tiny pools of water in the rocks are of blue-tinted loveliness, you do not weary of that walk along the shore.

I had seen a picture of the little town of Gudhjem, one that was entirely irresistible. No wonder, I thought, that when a house or two had been constructed and a name was necessary they had called it Gudhjem, which is God's Home. Parts of it are jotted by the rock-bound shore, while other parts lie scattered on the shoulder of a hill. Red is the prevailing colour of the place, but everywhere are trees, so that the roofs appear in all the foliage like some archipelago of joyous islands peeping out of the green, ruffled water. As you look on Gudhjem from outside it, either from the sea or land, it is so near the portrait of it painted by that artist who is not a Ruysdael nor a Hobbema—and does not have to be—that one can scarce forbear to cheer.

Some places, like some human beings, have extremely inappropriate names, because when they were christened it was not foreseen to what they would develop, but he was a genius who bestowed the name of Gudhjem. Here I must acknowledge with contrition that I did not search among the local archives to discover, if I could, the man's identity and other details of the gifted fellow. In the books on Bornholm there is not a single word about him and it may be that if I had studied every chronicle or document I would have lighted on no trace of him. Alas, how often we are told that we can leave with perfect confidence all matters such as fame and so forth to the judgment of posterity. One hopes that there was no such man and that the name of Gudhjem, even as a folk-song, was the work of many.

I could not investigate because the boat for Christiansö was on the point of leaving. Groups of people hurried down the narrow streets and more than one of them had beckoned to me or had shouted a kind warning. And I found myself with two men, one of whom—a tall man with a sparkling eye that shone out of a ravaged face—was telling his companion rather breathlessly about Tibet. He was good enough to interrupt himself and to inform me that we had no time for dalliance, as the harbour was in course of reconstruction, so that we would have to start the journey in a motor-boat from which they would transfer us to the steamer.

Then he told his friend, apparently a prosperous farmer, something more about Tibet. "Would you," he asked, "believe me if I were to say that I have seen a catechism taking place under a peach-forest in blossom while the snow-flakes fell?"

"I have seen nights in Bornholm," said the farmer, "which were made by God for His own happiness."

"In those Tibetan monasteries it is necessary for the catechized to sit down in a certain attitude and the questioner comes towards him with a rosary in his left hand. Afterwards the discussion begins, according to the rules of the logic of Nyaya. The questioner puts his queries with so much animation that, while he utters them, he beats time with his hands and feet. The teacher always instructs the catechists that the foot must come down so strongly that the door of hell may be broken open, and that the hands must make so great a noise that the voice of Knowledge may frighten the devils all over the world. What do you think of that?"

We managed to push our way into the motor-boat, although it looked as if it was completely full. And then the harbour-master came out of a temporary, very ramshackle building and one thought that he would tell the engineer to let her go. But he was the kind of man who feels that even an immoderate majority should act with moderation. A few other would-be passengers were running down towards the harbour, so he undid the rope which tied us to the bollard and refrained from leaving it, as he would otherwise have done, to trail behind us, for he slowly wound it into a neat circle.

Meanwhile a grey fog had crept up from the sea. It came so rapidly that people who were on the quay to see us off were very much like figures packed in cotton-wool. The steamer's horn was blowing and our whistle screamed. So they conversed with one another, proffering and taking good advice; experienced travellers, they did not minimize the peril we had to negotiate, a passage through the scattered rocks that one could hardly see. And then at last, the fog increasing heavily, the whole length of the ship—a mediocre length—remained invisible as we came to the side of her which had been opened to receive us.

On a table in the smoke-room were some copies of a guide to Christiansö, whose author I was very soon to meet and it was curious that he should be my second barber of this expedition. As I turned the pages of his little illustrated book I revelled in the detail of it. Obviously Sophus Bangs adores the island. Nothing would be here, I felt, inaccurate or slipshod. I compared it with a book which I had lately had to read, wherein another island, beautiful Majorca, was depicted; and the writer told us that "the wicked old Archduke Salvador of Austria" maintained a seraglio of some forty lovely girls, whereas the facts are that the Archduke Louis Salvator expended most of his fortune on scientific researches, published the results in handsome volumes decked out with his own engravings, and, as for his domestic affairs, he restricted himself rigidly to three ladies, as I was informed by the survivor of them.

My companions on the steamer did not interrupt me as I read the admirable Bangs. One does not expect that an island whose dimensions are a thousand feet by five hundred will have about it a great deal of history. Before the days of Christian V, who flourished at the same time as Charles II of England, no flag except perhaps that of the skull and cross-bones had ever been hoisted on this group of rocky isles far out in the Baltic. The pirates who infested those regions found Christiansö convenient, seeing that there is a smaller island, now called Frederiksö, a few yards from it and so situated that the intervening space is an excellent harbour. It could, and often did, accommodate no less than thirty vessels, those of the pirates and of their victims. On Christiansö the pirates would proceed to the division of the booty; a certain rock, the Rock of the Virgin, is still pointed out as the place from which a captured girl flung herself into the sea rather than become a part of the distribution. That is practically all we know concerning the little group previous to the year 1684.

Then it occurred to King Charles XI of Sweden that if he were to take them into his possession it would gravely incommode the pirates. Wachtmeister, one of his admirals, was at Karlskrona, a stronghold on the south-east coast of Sweden, and a messenger arrived from Charles with a despatch wherein the admiral was ordered to land upon those islands, annex them to the realm and place cannon here and there in suitable spots, adequate for the defence. Now Wachtmeister was the owner of a dog which had the privilege, the exclusive privilege, of entering his study whenever he wished to do so. This dog—we are not told about his breed, but his extraordinary intelligence would seem to prove that mongrel blood predominated in his veins—he noticed that this document upon his master's table was of much more interest than any of the other papers. So he took it out into the garden and examined it so energetically that he would have quite destroyed it if a body-servant of the admiral, by birth a Dane, had not come by and driven off the dog. He then deciphered what the King had written, after which he there and then decamped to Copenhagen and revealed the matter to his own King Christian V. Consequently it was this monarch and not King Charles whose emissaries annexed Christiansö, erected the circular citadel and built the stalwart battlements which are like cyclopæan walls. Two long barracks were constructed for a garrison of four hundred men and these yellow buildings, opposite each other, are to-day the village street. The commandant was provided with a house, part of which is now the one hotel and part the solitary shop. As for the hundred cannon that were set up on the island, they could never, as it turned out, be of use against the foe, but as a compensation they are still extant.

There was a booming through the fog, the voice of Christiansö. And as I went on deck to see if anything could be discerned, there among the other tourists were my two acquaintances and they were striding up and down, for it was cold.

"Here is something," said the farmer, "that you must not miss. That fog-horn, so he tells me, makes him think of the poor yaks."

The farmer thrust an arm through mine and I was promenading with the couple.

"Yes, that is so," said the tall man. "In the slaughter-houses of Tibet, when yaks are killed, the creatures have their legs tied in the yard amid the pools of blood from their dead comrades; tears are in their eyes, as if they know what will be done to them. Kawaguchi, the famous Japanese monk, said that he found the scene unbearable, and so did I; I mourned that I had not sufficient money to redeem their lives. And then a priest came in, carrying the Holy Texts; he read them for the doomed animal, on whose head the book and a rosary were placed. The natives believe that this ritual will allow the poor yak to enter into a new state of existence, also that it will absolve the doer of the cruel deed from evil consequences which might otherwise follow."

Then the fog permitted us to see the grey-green pyramid of Christiansö, whose summit is the lighthouse, and the lady who sold books and picture-cards in the saloon was at my side. One can lease a cottage in the rocks, she said, and for a price that is extremely low. She thought that there were seven or even eight artists living there, which is a good deal out of a total population of a hundred and twenty-nine.

"There," she said, "beyond Frederiksö, do you see that longish, hump-backed island? It is Graesholm—no one who is not a scientific ornithologist may land among those eider-ducks and seagulls. Formerly the Headman of the islands had the perquisite of gathering the plumage of those eider-ducks, but now they are left undisturbed. Which," she said, "is more than has been done for the inhabitants of Tat. You can just see it, granite blocks a foot or two above the water. Those who live there are the seals, and guns and ammunition are provided for the fisherfolk, because the seals are fond of eating fish, the salmon and the herring which these islanders exist upon. The Government would even pay so much for every seal, but now they do not pay. Ah, there is Sophus Bangs, that little hairy man. Let him know that you are not a tourist going back with us, that you want to be as much an islander as possible and he will help you."

"Mr. Bangs," I said, as I descended from the ship, saluted him and complimented him upon the book, "I hope to stay here for a week or so."

"Then you must see the Headman. He lives there, behind those trees."

"Does he decide," I asked, "who may remain? I will not even steal one apple from your Paradise."

"So long as you do not pluck many flowers," said Sophus Bangs, "because the soil would all get loose and ultimately it would be dispersed by the strong gales of winter."

CHAPTER VII

"NOW," said the buxom proprietress of the hotel, "as the ship has sailed away with all the tourists—did you notice how they liked to photograph each other sitting on our ancient cannons?—now that you are one of us it is necessary that you should visit Doctor Norman-Hansen at Mindet. The dear old gentleman—he is nearly eighty—will be in his garden, dictating to a girl the story of his life or else he will be writing the libretto of an opera."

"He loves to be disturbed?" I said.

Her smile was reassuring. "He does not show himself when all those people come," said she, "and that is only twice a week and only in the summer months, because it would be wearisome to sign his name so often. He is known all over Denmark, and beyond it too. But after they have sailed away he is most affable. Now go up to the backbone of the island and then down the other side."

I followed her instructions and within a grove of trees I came to Mindet, which means House of Memories. It was a black and white affair, as our memories are wont to be; large as houses go in Christiansö, but of the dolls' house style of architecture.

In the garden I concealed myself behind a tree, so that I should not interrupt a story that he was dictating, a grimly humorous adventure which had happened to him many years ago in Greenland. But my tree was not of a sufficient girth; the doctor noticed me and with the laughter of those quizzing eyes he put a stop to any awkwardness I felt. His other feature of most prominence was the luxuriant moustache.

" What can I do for you ? " he asked. " Some fruit and biscuits ? Let us help this amiable young woman with the branches of the mulberry."

We pulled them down while she collected the ripe, luscious fruit.

" You may have heard me talking about Greenland," he observed, " but one can be as happy here in Christiansö as anywhere. An old man is either much more or much less exacting. And how pleasant it is to feel that one can still be of some use. I am the doctor and the chemist and the midwife of this island and of Frederiksö. Professionally I am never overworked—the Ministry of the Marine in Copenhagen were benevolent to give me this appointment. They administer these islands. The pastor is appointed by them too. If anyone is ill I visit him for nothing, as if this were a ship. Oh, one can find far less desirable places. There are no rates and we pay in taxation about a tenth of what it amounts to on the mainland. By the way, the mainland for us here is Bornholm."

Meanwhile the secretary had come out with a plate full of biscuits, and we settled down to them and the mulberries.

" A few years ago," said the doctor, " we had an epidemic of measles. This young lady's brother brought it from Bornholm. He came over for a dance, and five-and-thirty people—adults, most of them—were victims. It was thirty years since there had been a case of it in Christiansö. Fortunately most of them had such a mild attack that chocolate pills were the chief medicine that I gave."

We spoke of many things. As for this island, said the doctor, it was one of the best places to get old in. One did not earn a great deal of money, thus one did not have the fear of losing it. He laughed as he remembered something. "Did you hear," he asked, "about that Syrian magnate? No? Then let me tell you. He was a very old and very rich man when he died. The biggest French official of the region called upon his family to sympathize. 'Votre père était un homme très digne,' he said. 'Ah oui, monsieur,' they answered. 'Et grand ami de la France.'—'Ah oui, monsieur.'—'Et presque centenaire.' —'Non, non,' they protested, 'presque millionaire.' . . . But even on this favoured island," said the doctor, "old age and prosperity are not synonymous. If you will walk with me I will be glad to show you a degenerate form of ivy. It is very ancient, very small and narrow in the leaf."

Some distance from the House of Memories we found ourselves upon the border of a cistern in the rocks. Large goldfish swam about in it. This was, he said, the islanders' supply of drinking water, replenished by the rain, as Christiansö does not possess a spring or an artesian well, and it would be too much to ask the island to support a river.

I was wondering why the goldfish could not be accommodated somewhere else.

"But no, they have a duty to perform," he said. "They have to eat all the impurities, the vegetable matter."

"And their own impurities?"

He shook his head. "Those are," quoth he, "quite unimportant. Let us sit down here and study the good fish. They have the strictest orders not to pay attention to the scraps of sausages and bread which tourists like to throw to them."

It was a very tranquil scene. Beyond the surface of the

water, silvery and of pale purple, one beheld—as now the fog had vanished—the long stretch of Bornholm, undulating on its way. The mighty sea-wall which the Danish soldiers had erected here on Christiansö with so much toil and furnished with a gateway here and there was not as useful now as it was picturesque. It would not have to be defended against anyone, I said.

"Who knows?" the doctor murmured. "Anyhow, it was not always so. I read of a young Scot, Captain Peter Henry Bruce, who landed here in 1724. He had served in Russia's army as an engineer, but had resigned and was returning to his native land. On June 28th he had embarked at Riga in the *Isabella*, and the conditions were so unfavourable that on July 10th the vessel had advanced no farther than the neighbourhood of Bornholm. From there she was driven back to Christiansö and struck upon a rock as she was entering the harbour. The commandant of Christiansö was a Colonel Hirschnach, who appears to have been a German, a professional soldier from one of the numerous German States. He perceived that Bruce was a passenger and sent his adjutant to invite him to step ashore. When Bruce and Hirschnach met they speedily discovered that they had faced each other in Flanders and in the vicinity of Copenhagen, when the Russians had invested the capital. Hirschnach may have been a gallant fellow, but he had no hobbies—none, at any rate, he could pursue upon our island—and he found that life was very tedious. Sometimes a whole year would elapse without one ship approaching them, save those which in the summer would occasionally come from Bornholm. Yet he himself had the resource of supervising his men when they landed on Graesholm to collect the feathers and eggs of the eider-duck, which brought him in about four hundred thalers a year."

"We were talking of the bastions," I said. "I do not understand why they might be required against the Scots. Surely there was no antagonism between that people and Denmark."

"But he had a Russian passport," said the doctor, "and

the Russians and the Danes were not on friendly terms. When Captain Bruce explained that he had left the Russian service he was shown in the most cordial manner what they would not otherwise have let him see, the details of the military works. They were, as he told them, in a lamentable state. Hirschnach agreed with him and before very long—after consulting with his brother-officer, Captain Fischer, and presumably with Mrs. and Miss Fischer—he urged the young man to remain at Christiansö, where his engineering skill would be much appreciated and he would, said the colonel, have no regrets. A marriage could be arranged with Captain Fischer's daughter, a pretty and charming girl eighteen years of age. But the Scot excused himself politely and on July 21st the *Isabella* sailed away. Captain, Mrs. and Miss Fischer bore the Scotsman no ill-will; they sent on board, addressed to him, provisions for the journey. As the *Isabella* had no cannon she fired a parting salute from seven muskets, which Christiansö acknowledged from several of her cannon."

" And Miss Fischer," I said, " what happened to her ? "

" Who knows ? " said the doctor. " But I can tell you a little more about Captain Bruce. He returned to Scotland, lived there for sixteen quiet years as a farmer and then put on a uniform again, this time on behalf of Britain against the Spaniards. He proceeded to the Bahamas as an engineer at thirty shillings a day, his duty being to help in the erection of a fort. After a time he became anxious to go back, for he had in Scotland a wife and, as he said, a ' pretty numerous flock of children.' "

The doctor then proposed we should inspect the narrow leaves of ivy he had told me of. And after that, what would I like to see?

" But I am taking up your time," I said.

" Ah, we are not the slaves of time," said he, " on Christiansö, though you must not imagine that the local intelligentsia—excuse the word—is idle. No, sir. As a rule we have more than one profession: the young clergyman, for instance, is likewise the schoolmaster; he conducts his class, when it is fine weather, in a field. Our

Headman is the magistrate, he is the customs-officer, while matters relating to salvage and old-age pensions are all in his hand. He and his wife are allotted the most imposing house of Christiansö with a suite of several rooms. Perhaps you saw it at the landing-place . . . No," said the doctor, as he took me by a short cut to the wall of ivy, leaping almost like a chamois from one boulder to another, " no, we are not idle here. Nor do we want to be, because the work of everyone is after his own heart, and with the women it is happily the same. One of our population is the postwoman; when the letters are sorted after the arrival of the motor-boat from Svaneke she puts on a scarlet jacket, which is her uniform, and then goes skipping round the island and to Frederiksö. Nobody has ever seen her read a post card, yet she is extremely well-informed."

Now we were in the presence of that ivy.

" Would it not be possible," said I, " to bring it back to life ? "

" A hundred years ago," the doctor said, " it was no doubt a lovely piece of vegetation."

" And it shall be so again," I said. " All that one has to do is to manure it. Then the leaves will——"

" They will never be restored to beauty."

" What we have to do," I said, " is to remove those brambles that keep off the sunlight and the rain."

" They can do nothing," said the doctor. " It will stay insensible to all their help."

" No, no, it will dance with them," I cried.

He stroked the shrivelled leaves.

" When we have nursed it back to life," I said, " and when the wind blows it will tremble."

" That is all the dancing it will ever do," said he. Then he set off at a rapid pace, climbing with such energy that very soon we had arrived where we could look down to the Headman's garden. There he was himself, a man of whom his Viking ancestors would have been proud.

Presently we joined him and, as we were strolling round the shadowed paths, one made allusion to his multifarious offices. But he made light of it. Not so long ago, he said, some eighty years, no lawyer could be found on Bornholm, which perhaps has got three or four hundred times the population of Christiansö. By this he did not mean that the Bornholmers were the kind of people who did not require a lawyer. More than one existed, but they each of them had other work as well. The leading lawyer of the island in the year 1855 was established at Rönne and he also held an office in connection with the militia, he sold books and cards and stamped paper. A little earlier than that there was only the regimental surgeon stationed at Rönne, and then in 1822 a young doctor came from Copenhagen and settled down at Nexö, the second largest town.

"But what happened to the people," I asked, "when they were ill?"

"If," said he, "it was that fever which they called the step-mother they were wont to treat it with a hearty dose of gunpowder. The remedy for colic was a tablespoon of pepper in half a glass of acquavit. Some of their ailments required a more elaborate medicine, such as one that was a mixture of burned hairs and the upper ends of stockings well dissolved in water, and this water had to be collected before sunrise from under a bridge and by a person who had not broken his fast. If you were to go to Graesholm you would find a grave dated 1685—it was then most rudimentary—a crowd of soldiers and workmen—no hospital, some hastily constructed huts and cholera patients lying anywhere."

"I for one would have rebelled," said a grey, quiet man who had just come into the garden. Afterwards I heard he was a member of a well-known family of manufacturers of china dogs and bowls and so forth who for many years have plied their trade in Rönne; he preferred a life less turbulent and for that reason has withdrawn to live upon the island.

"Is it possible," the doctor said, "for men to be good citizens who never were rebellious?"

"It may be," the Headman said to me, "that you have

not heard of our Dr. Dampe, a doctor of theology. If he had lived to-day he probably would have become a Member of Parliament. But he was born in 1790, and Denmark, now one of the most democratic of countries, had no Parliament until 1849. Dampe was imbued with advanced ideas ; he formed a brotherhood which called itself the ' Iron Ring.' They forbade him to preach—his sermons had been too political. Then he was sentenced to imprisonment for life. He lived for many years in that ochre-coloured house in Frederiksö. But he was a person of no great importance ; his punishment was much too severe and it is that alone which has caused him to be remembered."

The ex-manufacturer of china dogs remarked that other people had been incarcerated in that house.

Certainly, the Headman told him. A Swiss adventurer, who called himself Colonel Baron von Mueller d'Aarvangen, lived there for thirteen years on account of his transgressions in Copenhagen. Later on there came two Danish officers who, during 1848, went over to the rebels in Slesvig-Holsten. Most of the others were either duellists or else deserters. Some of them were allowed the freedom of the island, some of them escaped ; but even if they remained on Frederiksö they found it possible to mitigate their exile with gambling, drinking and fighting. Now for many years, he said, that house has had no inmate.

* * *

Some of us were sitting late that night upon the terrace that is built above the harbour. With the water laughing to us in the moonlight and the dome above us making a tent hung round with antique tapestries brought out for this occasion and the dark trees faintly touched with silver, on a night like this you felt that you were part of Christiansö's life.

" Are you not glad, my friends," said Doctor Norman-Hansen, " that your destiny has carried you to this dear island ? "

" I wish," said the ex-manufacturer of china dogs, " that

I could fill my soul with all the peace of it. Then I would be protected against everything."

"As for the nicest walks," said the proprietress of the hotel, "when I have time I will compose a list of them and hang it in the hall. What is your feeling with regard to coloured splotches that they put on trees? Myself, I rather deprecate them. Owing to my occupation—we keep open all the year—I have not had the chance of being an explorer. And besides——" She looked down at her ample figure.

"Not at all!" I said. "So long as fortitude and enterprise are there one can be just as brilliant an explorer as the next person."

"Really, do you think——?"

"But who," I said, "can doubt it? You would have become a grand explorer."

"What I think," said she, "is this: to find oneself in trackless jungles or in wastes of iceberg with no indication, naturally, of the way and then to work it out by means of your deductive wisdom, your—what joy could equal it? So let us not spoil the paths of Christiansö. I say that if you are the kind of man who has a brain you are insulting God if you do not make use of it."

We were impressed by her emotion and the barber-author, little Sophus Bangs, was saying that he grieved because the clergyman was not amongst us. What she had put forward with respect to God would very much have interested him, said Sophus Bangs.

"I myself," said the accommodating lady, "will repeat it him to-morrow if you like. And I am glad that we will not have coloured signs upon our trees and rocks. As I have told you, it has not been possible for me to go exploring in the trackless jungles and among those icebergs; but in a damp, foggy night I can be somewhere on this island and have all the breathless joy of being lost. Then it is that the explorer in me would attack the problems. I would have to use all my sagacity."

"If," said the lighthouse-man—it was his weekly night of leave when he was able to indulge in Christiansö's dissipation, a long talk upon the terrace—" if you would use your compass——"

"Now, young man," she said, and rather viciously, "I am the owner of the shop, as you are well aware, and we do not have compasses for sale. There comes a time," said she, a note of triumph in her voice, "when you can lean on your exploring qualities. But when I make my expedition there are people," she was looking grimly at the lighthouse-man, "whom I will not take with me."

"I believe," he said, undaunted by her fell decision or, perhaps, endeavouring to recover his repute in the esteem of Christiansö, as if no dreaded punishment had been pronounced against him, "but I am not sure," he said, "that we shall not have rain. Please wait and I will run up there and read the forecast."

It would have been utterly discourteous to the island had I pointed out that in a place of those dimensions we could run to the hotel without much damage from the rain in whatsoever part it might befall us. But I told the lighthouse-man that I was well informed as to the weather and that we could safely start upon our stroll.

At any rate, we were no worse off than the readers of the "Galignani Messenger," the newspaper in English that was published certain years ago in Paris. Every night before it went to press the editorial staff, who numbered four (one of them a friend of mine), would gaze—or one or two of them—out of the window. Then they would deliver to the printer what the forecast was for the next day; it was the result, they wrote, of observations made by Galignani's special staff of weather experts.

There was no discussion as to which part of the islands we should make for. The narrow, iron bridge to Frederiksö, that swings aside when necessary, was intact when we arrived, because the herring-boats—the anchorage of most of them is on the west side of the bridge—would not go out for some time with the nets. And so we came to Frederiksö and to some waste land in between the scattered houses. Across the water to the left of us lay the dark shape of Graesholm. Her inhabitants were not all wrapped

Svaneke, the little Port

The Smoking of Herrings on the Waterfront

Nylars Church, showing the Murals which are noted for their fine Colour Combinations, the Decorative Borders being particularly attractive. The Artist's technique, however, is primitive and his religious conceptions naïf

Nylars Church, dating from the 12th Century

in sleep, for one could hear a squawk arising now from this point now from that, and then a solitary bird would start into the air and seek another lodging for the night. From the angry noise they made it seemed improbable that they were setting out to their inamoratas, but that they were flying from them and the rage of husbands.

CHAPTER VIII

I GOT up next morning at a quite unwonted hour. Down in the port there was a scene of great activity. Along the quay of Frederiksö were rather more than half a dozen vessels and about four people, men and women, were at work on each of them. What they were doing was to extricate the fish, a tedious operation, from the net; one party stayed on board their boat, the neighbouring one preferred to do the job upon the quay—the disadvantage of unloading all the heavy nets was compensated by the greater elbow-room on shore. But whether they selected one mode or the other they were equally at peace with the whole world. Most of the men were smoking pipes and there was a continuous flow of merry talk, the women being evidently glad to feel that they had fingers no less agile than the men's.

As I was watching one of these quartettes who gossiped to their hearts' delight while never pausing in the work they had to do—save when a pipe had to be filled or when a net was emptied of its captives and another one had to be draped about the horizontal bar—as I was watching these contented people I perceived that it was not because of an unusual catch, for they were joined by two men just as happy as themselves and these two had returned to port with such a modest cargo that they had transferred the whole of it already into boxes which at seven o'clock would leave for Svaneke.

" Well, mister," said a jovial, thick-set person who was in another boat. He flung a herring—one that was not large enough to keep—into the water and immediately there was a swooping and a lucky seagull of the multitude which darted here and there fled from his comrades with the prey. " You should have got up earlier," said the fisherman, " and come with us to bring the nets in. It was only twenty minutes out to sea."

Then he related how, as boy and man, he had been in so many English vessels and he once had spent three days in Cardiff and a day at Newcastle-on-Tyne. Oh yes, he knew the language quite all right.

Opposite to him his well-upholstered wife was working at the net, and proudly she surveyed her man. Nor was he unwilling to display his knowledge. If I wished to hear concerning Newcastle-on-Tyne, he said, he would be pleased to tell me a good deal.

" I should imagine that it is much more enjoyable," I said, " upon this island."

" We are well off," said the fisherman. " On Mondays we are paid, the rate is good and now we have the wireless, everything we want."

The seagulls wanted more. They had increased the shrillness of their exclamations. But the company of eider-ducks were not obtrusive, passing to and fro upon the water in the hope that breakfast would descend upon them or so near to them that the swift seagulls would not crash from overhead and seize it. Such a clamour did the seagulls make that I was on the verge of shouting.

" You all seem," I said, " to be a happy band of people."

" Over there," he pointed with his pipe, " is what we call the Moon, that simple, yellow house. But as it is the largest one on Frederiksö you will have noticed it."

I shook my head. " When I was here last night, I told him——"

" Last night it was not illuminated," said the fisherman. " It really is the House of Commons or the Council Chamber of this island, or the Parish Hall, but those meetings are soon over and they are not often held. The Moon is where we dance, it has a nice harmonium for the music. And what nights we have when Danish warships come to Christiansö or when we have a visit from a foreign fishing fleet."

Perhaps his wife had never heard him make so long and eloquent a discourse in the English language. She was beaming on him, on their fellow-workers and on me. She could not have looked more thrilled if upon her busy hands the herring-scales had magically turned to silver.

He was noticing that I was rather disconcerted by the noise of all those gulls. "They are like that," he said, " it can't be helped. And we," he said disarmingly, " we chatter too."

I mentioned that the conversation in a lonely place in West Australia I had heard of occupied itself, more frequently than not, with an old murder, one which happened in the nineteenth century. Had they in Frederiksö more recent subjects for their gossip?

He replied that all things change. His father used to say that it was customary in his youth to put the coffee-cups into the cupboard as they were and wash them on a Saturday. The coffee was not made of coffee, but of peas and rye.

"Talking about food," I said, "why does one see no eider-drakes upon the water?" Everyone, apparently, was female, brown and undistinguished.

"That is true," said he as he glanced round, "the sons and husbands are not here. And why?"

His colleague, who was loitering upon the quay because the catch that he had taken was exiguous, this colleague leaped into the breach. He said the males were all on Graesholm. "You can see them there," he said, "with beautiful white backs, behind their heads a pale green plumage and black feathers on the top of it. And they are proud, they will not demean themselves to snatch the food that man has thrown away."

Gradually the long, wooden boxes had received their complement of fish; beside the bridge was a machine for weighing them. And on a wheelbarrow they were transported to the other island where the shapely motor-boat, whose name is Svaneke, was waiting to set out. One third of the crew had oiled her engine and he saw to it that every box was properly bestowed around the deck. The sea gave promise of remaining calm, so that there was no need to put the merchandise for safety in the hold.

My friend the fisherman presented me with half a dozen herrings. They had been alive, he said, two hours ago. And they would live, he thought, a long time in my memory.

His colleague said that larger ones existed in the world, but if you only like the large things . . .

" These islands ! "

" That is so," he said.

A blast came issuing from Svaneke, her siren, but although it had a peremptory sound, that was because the siren could not modulate its voice. On this occasion what it meant to say was that the boat would leave in thirty minutes, if not later.

Presently my fisherman had done his morning's work, the boxes were despatched and we went over to the boat. By this time the remainder of the crew had put in their appearance and the landing-place began to have an air of some activity. One saw, for instance, Christiansö's handsome priest who was about to sail to Bornholm, where he would be meeting all his brothers of the Church in conclave. Then the chambermaid of the hotel turned up, she had a list of things that the proprietress required. And then we saw the postwoman who brought the bag of letters from that office in the upper storey of the house some fifty yards away. She had arrayed herself in her official scarlet jacket.

" All her life," observed the colleague, " has been faithfully devoted to the post office of Christiansö and there must never be the slightest stain upon it."

" If any bandits were to make a raid upon her office," said the fisherman, " and have a boat to carry them away, I know that she would rush off to the Headman, so that he should fire a cannon at them."

"Poor old cannon," said the colleague, "they have had their day. Once when the enemy appeared we fired a mortar, but the man who knows all that is Doctor Norman-Hansen. You had better ask him if you want to know. The mortar broke in two when it was fired, but nobody was killed."

When I applied to Norman-Hansen he explained it all. "It happened," he said, "in October 1808. After a good deal of hesitation, as it was a very aged piece, the soldiers settled to make use of it against their foe, the British warships, who remained at such a distance that our cannon took no part in this engagement. When the mortar burst in two one half was flung on to the rocks beside the harbour and the other half across our island to the south. We prudently refrained from firing any other mortars; we remembered the prophetic words : "One woe doth tread upon another's heels, so fast they follow." A number of the garrison might have been killed and they were lucky to escape with one man wounded. They had still more reason to congratulate themselves on the bombardment from the ships, seeing that so many shells were aimed at them and the bombardment lasted for about five hours and only seven soldiers lost their lives. The others were relieved. That little book by Sophus Bangs says that six of them were Swedes imprisoned in that house in Frederiksö where Doctor Dampe lived so long. The six were playing cards when they were instantaneously killed."

I said it was surprising that the ships did not do greater damage.

"The commander of the ships was discontented too," said Norman-Hansen.

"But how could he know that he was having such a moderate success," I asked, "if he did not come nearer to the land?"

"A big proportion of the shells were falling in the sea and others on the isle of Graesholm where no people lived. He sent a vessel to the west of Christiansö and when it signalled what was happening the shells began to be much less innocuous, they ricochetted from the rocks, so that the fragments flew in all directions. But I have to go," the doctor said. "I wish I could have told you more—I made a special study of this one engagement we have had—however, I must not neglect my daily duty."

If I could go with him, I proposed, to the consulting-room and leave, of course, if any patient were to come. . . .

He put his arm through mine and off we hurried, halting only at the little custom-house to see the copy of a picture painted by a Frenchman who by chance was present on that fateful day of 1808. The picture shows that a good many ships were in the harbour, but they were not of a kind to disconcert the British vessels.

Then as we were sitting in the very neat consulting-room, which at the same time is a chemist's shop, the doctor said that I might not exactly know what the conditions in the Baltic were when Christiansö's peaceful period was interrupted. So he offered to fill in the picture for me. In 1808 Britain's one ally in the Baltic was Sweden, for Napoleon had now induced the Russians to take part in his blockade of Britain. The Swedish King, Gustavus Adolphus, was alarmed, so that an adequate naval and military force came out from England to protect him. The *Victory*, which had been thoroughly repaired after Trafalgar, was commissioned at Chatham early in March for Sir James, subsequently Lord, de Saumerez's flag. His fleet amounted to 62 sail, ships of the line, sloops and gun-vessels. The admiral's orders were that he should attempt to destroy the Russian fleet and afford protection to the King of Sweden. The Swedes, according to the great Sir John Moore, who was in command of the soldiery, were both brave and upright; but Gustavus Adolphus made to Sir John several absurd proposals, such as an attack on Copenhagen and Cronstadt, for which his force was insufficient. When Sir John refused the King commanded him to stay in Stockholm. It was necessary for the general to escape from this peculiar ally by means of a ruse; he begged permission to send his aide-de-camp, Colonel Graham, to the admiral with despatches, and he himself made the journey, wearing the colonel's uniform. It happened that one year later Gustavus Adolphus was likewise told to remain in Stockholm and by his own people. He was dethroned; as evidence of the condition of his mind a paper of his was published which they found on his desk. Therein he described himself as the man on the white horse in the Book of the Revelation and announced that he must fight a battle under the walls of Copenhagen, for the purpose of bestowing perpetual peace on Europe. . . . " Well, now," said the doctor, "I found in the Record Office in London that de Saumerez wrote to the Admiralty that ' these islands have been reported to me to be strongly fortified, particularly——' "

Christiansö is a friendly place and as the lighthouse-man had then no very urgent task he came to the consulting-room. He said that he was glad to find me there as he had always wanted me to see the lighthouse.

" We are in the middle of a battle, so to speak," I said. " Would you not like to listen? It is that one fought in Christiansö more than a hundred years ago."

" With all my heart," said he, as he sat down upon the chair you can adjust for patients to lie horizontally.

" Where was I? " asked the doctor. " Yes, I recollect —de Saumerez reported that particularly the tower on the summit of our island is so strongly fortified that it is represented to be bomb-proof, and he doubted much whether this archipelago could be reduced without a considerable land force being disembarked under cover of line-of-battle ships. No further communication on the subject of Christiansö appears to have reached the British Admiralty; perhaps de Saumerez made no report because he did not consider his bombardment from such a distance was a very glorious action."

" And after that," said I, " these islands had no further part in warfare? "

" That is so," said Norman-Hansen. " Christiansö returned to peaceful ways, but the communications were uncertain, the amenities restricted and the troops could not endure the dullness. In 1809 about 200 of them rebelled, took ship to Sweden and enrolled in the Swedish army. A garrison continued to be kept on Christiansö, but after some years it was withdrawn and the barracks were placed at the disposal of the fishermen and others."

The lighthouse-man with an effort raised himself out of the chair which had become a couch. He said that one can always learn and he would not forget what Dr. Norman-Hansen had been telling us. He personally felt, he said, as pleased as a grey plover which has thrust its beak into the sand and come upon a city full of insects. Now, he thought, we might be going to the lighthouse.

"It may be," the doctor said, " that you have heard about the man who rendered thanks to God for having got so far and he did not know where he was."

We left the doctor at his post and this time we did not go by the route of the hotel, but we ascended to the higher ground by that long, winding flight of steps, so quaint and so irregular and such a solace for the islanders, as was explained to me by my companion.

" There was a person here," he said, " who told us that the steps are perfectly Italian, like those that lead up to the hillside chapels or that take you up past the Stations of the Cross."

Dappled sunlight through the trees, among them fig-trees, fell upon those grey, uneven steps. It was a lovely scene, but as a number of the steps had in the course of years been broken off and left in that condition you were forced to watch them carefully or you would also come to grief.

" So if you wish," observed the lighthouse-man— " wish to pretend you are in Italy you walk a little up and down the steps."

There is a kind of interval when you are half-way up and to the right, in ambuscade behind the most luxuriant shrubs, there is a rambling, chocolate-coloured house where one of Christiansö's painters—this one an extraordinary portrait-painter—lives. His model and her brother were engaged in peeling some potatoes in the garden.

" One thing," said the lighthouse-man, as we were starting on the second flight of steps, " that I would like to have explained to me is this—what do they do in Italy when they want to pretend they are in Christiansö?"

CHAPTER IX

BEFORE one can be naturalized—I think it is the general demand in European and non-European countries—one must be a resident for several years. A notice has to be inserted in the papers and I daresay that enquiries will be made as to your conduct in your land of origin. No doubt some fees will also be extracted from you. But how much more genial and more generous are the Christiansö proceedings. They are swift and yet are imperceptible. You do not wake up one morning and discover that you are included in the family, for that would be too sharp a contrast with the person you were yesterday. The Headman of the islands does not issue any document, so that it is impossible in after years to give the date of your felicity. What happens is that you glide into it. The Headman would not dream of asking any questions; he and all the other islanders perceive that you are worthy. That is all they ask.

Once you are naturalized the days on Christiansö dissolve in one another. What you recollect of them does not fall into separate compartments, this the deed of Monday, this the meditation which you had on Tuesday. But as you have been received into the life of Christiansö, so do you mingle with it your own life. You two are interwoven. That is why there is no sequence in my other days upon the island:

Walking past the cistern where the goldfish cleanse the water that we drink I meet the pastor's wife and little girl —we talk about the water's goodness and about the goldfish who secure it and themselves may sicken. How should they be treated? "Ordinary goldfish," says the pastor's wife, "will often free themselves from some indisposition if salt water is provided for them, one-fifth of the water being salt. But how can that be done with water that the population drinks?" The little girl is anxious to throw something in and is so tactfully prevented by her mother that she does not seem to suffer any disappointment. . . . Nets are spread upon the stones of Frederiksö to dry. . . . The charming cemetery near the Headman's garden with a few majestic sepulchres of granite, on them the armorial bearings of a commandant, his wife and other folk who flourished in the far-off time when Christiansö was called by Nelson the Malta of the Baltic. . . . At two o'clock each afternoon the motor-boat returns from Svaneke and in the harbour everybody is complacent, for they know that they will carry parcels home and maybe there will be an unexpected one. A member of the crew is in the hold, from there he flings or hands the merchandise, acording to its nature, and his comrade on the deck completes the operation and calls out the name of the recipient. Even those things that come every day, such as the cans of milk or loaves of bread, are made most welcome. Universal interest is displayed when parcels come ashore of which the contents are uncertain—thus for a gaunt fisherman there is produced a greenish, wooden case with " Medicine " written plainly on a label, but as neither he nor yet his family are ill those bottles will become one of the major topics of the town. . . . The church that usually is locked, but as the windows are not made of coloured glass you can look through them and inspect the treasures : the curved candelabra that once hung inside the royal yacht, the pastel on the altar that supplies a tenderness to what would be too stern an atmosphere, and if you have good eyesight you will revel in the rich embroidered cloth of red and gold, sewn and presented by the daughter of an admiral. . . . The circular and lofty citadel which rises over Christiansö, the Latin tablet at the entrance with its proud inscription to " the best and greatest " monarch, Christian the Fifth. In resounding phrases we can learn what he accomplished, he who in the wars, so we are told, could not be overcome and who in battle with the elements, the fury of the sea, the raging wind, would be the conqueror, and how he could not even be intimidated by the most ferocious works of nature, the terrific rocks of Christiansö, but that upon this island he had built a fortress which was perfectly impregnable. The British naval officer who came upon the scene more than a century after this and warned the Admiralty that the citadel was bomb-proof, he did not sail near enough to read those Latin words, so that it seems the fame of them had spread. How pleasant is the tale of this affair for those of us who deal in words. . . . A writer frequently in Christiansö was Holger Drachmann, one of Denmark's greater poets. Standing on the citadel, he said that when you see from there how the horizon is round, the island is round, the citadel round and that you are round, you almost feel as if you were the axle round which everything revolves. . . . There is a great deal more that you will carry with you out of Christiansö. Those who have lived there cannot be like other folk again. To tell you the particulars would be most reprehensible, for one should not unveil those mysteries. And you would be burned up with envy.

When the day arrived for me to go down to the quay and to embark, there was a more than usual commotion, for the Headman had to go to Bornholm. He was walking up and down, involved in very earnest conversation with the pastor and with Dr. Norman-Hansen. It seemed obvious that they, and possibly some other islanders, had been allotted the administration of the Headman's miscellaneous duties and he was now giving them a final word of sage advice, so that this period of interregnum might be safely traversed. Just before we started the proprietress of the hotel, whose very moderate bill, save for an item here and there, had been made out in English, hurried down to ask me to accept a basket of provisions, very necessary, so she said, as we would be at sea for two whole hours.

We left at a good speed and turned at such an angle to the island group that Christiansö and Frederiksö were merged in one, but Graesholm we could still discern. Some emissaries of its population hovered round us, for they knew we had on board the Headman, and their island is included in his realm. As for the seals on distant Tat, there was no sign of them, for they were registering a protest. Liberty is the inheritance of all upon the other islands, whether they be human-beings, eider-ducks or gulls. Christiansö and Frederiksö and Graesholm have what is no bubble reputation, for they are oases in a rather naughty world, delightful haunts where freedom takes her ease. But on the isle of Tat prevails, in the opinion of all those who dwell there, a most evil persecution. And the Headman of the group, the King of Denmark's representative, has never raised his voice against the slaughter of the seals of Tat, indeed he justifies it on the ground that they consume the salmon and the herring. Never has a seal denied that these are what he lives upon, and is it not unseemly and illogical, they say, for anyone to wish to blame them for it while not taking steps to place a menu of some other kind before them? There is a decisive difference, declare the Tatians, between themselves who live a good deal on the land, those granite rocks, so that as islanders they should be granted the same freedom as the others, and those poor fish that have no earthly home. That is why they look askance upon the Headman, and when he proceeds on leave they do not furnish any kind of escort.

When the birds had executed their manœuvres, all accompanied with music, they joined in a final chorus, after which, obedient to the protocol, they gracefully withdrew.

"Now do you think," the Headman was remarking, "that it is among the wisest observations of Confucius when he tells us that the higher type of man will seek within himself what he requires, while the inferior man will search for it in others?"

If he was alluding to the absence of the seals, as I presumed, then it appeared to me that he was taking it in a most creditable fashion; I determined to approximate as closely as I could to him in tact while paying tribute to his manifold arrangements, so that his departure should not cause those islands to become a scene of dire confusion.

"No doubt you will always let them know," I said, "where you are to be found, so that if a problem should arise they can refer to you."

"I shall not be in touch with them till I return," he said.

"You have such faith," I asked, "in their discretion and their judgment? They do not possess your knowledge of the art of governing. And if they have to solve a real problem——"

"It can wait," the Headman said, "for I am going back at twelve o'clock."

Then I retired into another part of the small boat and wrote this little piece:

> When we are torn away
>   From a beloved spot
> Where the most happy day
>   Has fallen to our lot,
> Woe be to us, we cry,
> We that are doomed to die,
> For now we have to pass
> Like shadows on the grass.
>
> O will the grass not shake,
>   Though winds be wrapped in sleep
> And there is none awake?
>   It has a watch to keep,
> Because where love came down
> Becomes a holy town—
> Years fly, years fly and yet
> The grass will not forget.
>
> From Paradise we fare
>   At the command of fate—
> Let us not in despair
>   Sit weeping at the gate.
> The glories we beheld
> Will never be expelled
> From us, but of our heart
> Will be a precious part.

* * *

Petersen was acting in the most extraordinary fashion. While our boat was entering the harbour he stood underneath a crane and waved his hat, which was a very reasonable thing to do. But as we chugged our way into the inner basin I could see distinctly that his legs were dancing, though he looked as if he was unconscious of it. And as I ran up the steps and shook his hand he laughed so oddly that—was it a case of sunstroke or was this the usual conduct of the egg and butter merchant which he had concealed from me in those few days before we took our separate paths from Rönne?

On our way to the hotel we glanced upon each other sideways—it was really quite embarrassing—and with respect to those Round Churches he had uttered not a word.

"Tell me, Petersen," I said, "your quest, has it been satisfactory? You know, that paper you are going to read in England—those Round Churches."

"If I had not been looking at the splendid Nyker, that is Newchurch, which was new seven hundred years ago, then I would never—there is something I must tell you!"

"It is clear," I said, "that you have not confined your interest to very ancient things. Is it a serious affair?"

By this time we were in the most extensive courtyard I had seen in Bornholm. As the builders of the railway had not thought it worth while to connect their system with this little town, why should it have a hostelry of such imposing size? Some twenty carriages could be assembled in that sandy courtyard. Was it that the place had been frequented once by many pilgrims owing to some cavern in the neighbourhood in which a saint had lived, and by the time the railway was constructed other saints were being honoured?

At the threshold of the house I saw that in the office to the right there sat a very large, good-natured-looking person.

"Ah," said he to Petersen, "your friend has come. I shall be pleased to have the latest news of Christiansö. And you can both have rooms with eastern aspect, which are much preferred by everyone, for you can look out on the harbour and the life of Svaneke."

We followed him upstairs and he was quite indifferent to the fact that not one of the upper rooms was occupied. He did not say, as many others would have done, that they were all reserved for people whom he was expecting in a day or two.

"Let me bid you welcome to my house," he said. "My name is Werth, Thor Werth."

Maybe that was the reason of the man's indifference as to

the patronage accorded him. His godly name, perhaps, exerted on him such effect that he could take no part in ordinary mundane struggles, he could not descend to running after clients or to saying that he had them when he had them not. The courtyard also may have been constructed by a person with a name of grandeur and the resolution to deserve it.

Now, said Mr. Thor, he would conduct us personally to a few of Svaneke's main glories. So he led the way downstairs, through several public rooms (of which the public were omitting then to take advantage) and into the strip of garden dominated by the famous mulberry.

"We have been forced," he said, "to fasten round my poor old friend this iron band. Think of how it suffers—and these various supports, these crutches that prevent it from collapsing. Out of all its agony it gives to us the sweetest berries in the world. Before we go into the town please eat a few of them. I would not like the tree to be offended."

Then as we debouched upon the sandy market-place he said it was a pity we had not arrived the day before and listened to Professor Jörgensen of Copenhagen. "He goes everywhere," said Mr. Thor, "and talks of agriculture. We have had philanthropists and, ever since the year 1769, The Farmers' Economic Association arranges for the sons of farmers to receive a very thorough education first in one kind of farm and then in another."

"Excellent," I said, "but why should you be sorry that we missed him?"

"Oh, well, well," said Mr. Thor. "But I do hope that when you see our windmill it will gratify you."

There was at this hour no single stall remaining in the market-place. Two errand-boys rode simultaneously into it on bicycles and, as they both were members of the haute école, they had to act as if the place was totally obstructed, leaving only the most narrow passage for themselves. By superhuman skill they managed to avoid a clash. Yes, they were artists.

And as it happened Mr. Thor was telling us about another

artist who had looked at their old windmill, parts of which go back three hundred years. This artist said it would have been more friendly to break up the windmill rather than to leave it here to listen to the wind. For when the wind calls and it would endeavour to go racing with it as in other days we tie it down, we torture it, the artist said, and that he was surprised to have to tell them that.

Mr. Thor glanced at the windmill somewhat furtively. " We had sixty-three," he said, " in Bornholm at the beginning of the nineteenth century. I do not know, I do not know," he faltered, " if we really did deserve them. Most of them were little ones that could be moved from place to place."

He left us and I was informed by Petersen about the girl whom he was going to marry. It had been a wrench for him to come away from her, but he had done so for two reasons, firstly to fulfil his undertaking with me, secondly because she had commissioned him to find a place in the Paradisbakkerne, the Paradise Hills, where they would spend their honeymoon. These hills were, he told me, between Svaneke and Nexö.

Thus when Mr. Thor that evening said he did not know if we should go beside the sea and have enjoyment of the rocky bays and of the curious monoliths in several places, or if we should take the inland route, by the famous Paradise Hills, we were not long in making up our minds.

And when we started, early the next day, the scattered clouds were being blown across a sky profoundly blue, and as we made our way along a road with not a wall nor hedge in sight the wind was dancing round us in a boisterous fashion. Now and then, but at long intervals, there was a farm-house situated a few hundred yards away from the straight road. It seemed as if this road had been constructed so that no one of the farmers should have more advantage from it than his neighbours.

Far off, in front of us, upon an elevated piece of ground, we could discern a clump of buildings with a very large, white church and belfry in the midst of them. We had been told in Svaneke that this was the obscure hamlet of Ibskirke.

But there had been a time when the inhabitants of Svaneke were forced to keep an eye upon the sea, from which they were attacked by pirates and nefarious men. That was why so many of their windmills had been portable, adapted to the needs of persons who at any moment might have to decamp. At Ibskirke they were comparatively safe from the attentions of the pirates; still, the walls of that church, too, are very thick.

One of the stones erected in the churchyard was to someone who had died in 1882, and he had been both a lieutenant in the army and a man in the police. In which of his professions had he been of greater service to the State?

There sidled up to us a very aged gardener whose frame was almost as contorted as a venerable olive-tree. When he had wished us, very pleasantly, good-morning, he stood propped upon his rake, prepared to be of any help.

"Oh yes, I knew that man," he said. "When he was in the world he was a farmer, Farmer Ipsen. Yes!"—he suddenly burst into merriment—"I did not think of it till now," he said. "That Ipsen cultivated a good deal of land, but I have only this." He waved a claw-like hand round his domain.

"Well, thank you very much," said Petersen, "we must be going now. We have a long way still before us."

"No," he chuckled, "it is not so long as that. There are roads to heaven and hell. If you would like to be directed I will——"

Petersen was on the move, pretending that he did not hear him. I, however, stopped. This old man fascinated me, apart from that extremely useful information he was offering to give.

Those travellers are supermen who, being told the way with many details they are asked to bear in mind, have not let their attention wander. The results, if one should not be able to enquire again, are liable to prove disastrous; and the gardener was well aware of this. He felt afraid, good fellow that he was, that we would so confuse the matter as to take of his two roads the wrong one. Therefore, being wise no less than kindly, he did not endeavour to sketch out for us a path to follow. He did not refer again to those two destinations, heaven and hell.

"If you want to go," said he, "to Nexö you can walk along the road or else upon the green path through the hills. We all are very fond of them."

CHAPTER X

SPEAKING for myself, the walk became a little less enjoyable as we approached the woodland. I began to doubt the wisdom of the persons who had given to the district such a title. We possess, of course, in cities very sordid and repulsive thoroughfares equipped with a celestial or a lovely name; if one encounters, say, a Paradise Building or a Paradise Row that are situated in a slum, we know that the city fathers, taking to heart the advice of their Goethe, who says that we should tell a man he is what we hope he will become, we know that they have given those high names in order that the population shall believe that all is for the best in the best possible of worlds.

When, however, such a name of glory is bestowed upon a part remote from towns, when it has been given by the neighbours of a wilderness because of their unbounded admiration for it, then a stranger coming to the district feels that probably it is a chance of one to thirty-three that he will think the name is justified. How much more sensible, he says, it would have been to make an understatement, leaving it for others to enlarge upon it. Such a name as Hills of Paradise—how can it fall upon a traveller's ear with any favourable sound? You will be asking what persuaded me to come this way, since I had not the same romantic reason as Knut Petersen. I have no answer save that I am human, one who does not only kill the thing he loves but loves the thing that kills him and will be attracted by what he will want to fly from. Hills of Paradise forsooth!

The road that we were walking on, an unpretentious road between ploughed fields, brought us to the buildings of a farm; a portion of it was devoted to the tourist traffic—quite a lot of little tables were assembled in a room and others underneath the trees. When we had been waiting near a tree about five minutes a myrmidon came wandering rather casually up to us and asked if we had any wishes. This apparent indifference was not caused by the fact that there was no rival establishment. I am certain that the proprietor wanted us, in the first place, to feel at home, to become acclimatized before being disturbed.

After we had taken some refreshment, there was put before us by the maid a large map of the Hills of Paradise. The territory seemed to be divided into many ranges and of course they run in various directions.

"Here," she said, as she brought down her thumb into the middle of the map, " here is the celebrated rocking-stone and you can reach it either this way "—and she traced a devious route—" or by some other ways if you prefer." It would be better if we were to follow the red marks and if at some uncertain point we could not see one, we must then go to the next point where we could. " I hope," she said, " the track you take will always be the right one. All the little valleys have their names."

One might hope these valleys would be so intelligent that if you shout at one of them there would be a sonorous echo, but if on the other hand the name you shout is not the one to which the valley answers all one's shouts would be received in silence.

" Do the people often lose themselves ? " I asked.

" They usually are of this part of the island," said the maid. She added in the kindest fashion that it would have pleased her to go with us, but she had been left alone to serve the guests, because the other people of the farm were occupied. " But if you do not see the rocking-stone," said she . . .

When she was gone in search of something else for us we hastily conferred. We had to see the rocking-stone, that was essential. Though she had not said it in so many words her voice had made it very clear that if we failed to see this natural phenomenon there would be not much reason for us to continue to exist. If after travelling through the Hills of Paradise we had to make confession that we had not seen the rocking-stone we might as well have mill-stones hung about our necks.

The maid compelled us to write down the names of several valleys and her honest face was full, in fact too full, of confidence when we departed. Evidently she had sworn a solemn vow that she would hide from us her deep misgivings.

We were in a sort of lane with boulders underfoot, they had been painted red quite lavishly, here in this corridor where it would be impossible to lose oneself.

The path led up a brief incline with clumps of heather. But the stones were large and practically flat, which made it possible for us to go at a good rate. They looked as if they had been thrust into the ground by giants who had set about the paving of the district. Now and then we had to hop from one stone to another, yet our progress was not slow and with the red paint still quite prominent we had no kind of trouble.

There was one place where the path divided into two that were of equal size and of importance, it would seem, and here no paint was visible. Perhaps the rain had washed it out or else a person hostile to the sort of man whose path in life had been too easy. We had now to use our judgment, instinct, luck, intelligence and any other ally we could summon. And we chose correctly, for when we had gone some fifty yards a red mark on a tree sang out to us.

"I feel," said Petersen, "that very soon we shall be expert woodmen. I had no idea we had it in us."

We were striding through a valley of an oblong shape with a grey-yellow wall of cliff at one side; facing it there was a more uneven wall of earth and heather. Then the path went serpentining upward till it disappeared in a round, muddy space where sawn-off parts of trees were waiting to be dragged away. Of course one could distinguish instantly the road which had been taken by their predecessors and no other path could be discerned. It might be that the wood was being shipped along a route which happened to go past the rocking-stone. At any rate, it was a wide and comfortable track.

Then we were going down an ordinary lane. A motor-car was at a gate, beside it stood a man.

We asked him if we had come through the Hills of Paradise. One had imagined that it was a more extensive district where, unless you be a native, you could easily be lost. We told him of the farm from which we had begun this expedition.

" Then," he answered, " you have not been through the Hills, for you have only skirted them. There is a lot you have not seen—cliffs, valleys, gorges, heather, granite and all that, a kind of labyrinth of rock and tree. Yet in the world there are some parts more savage——"

" That," I said, " I can believe."

" Not much more savage," said the man. " You could not plant the smallest thing to be of any use."

" He would be foolish who would try," said Petersen.

" Well, my master knows the Hills of Paradise from one end to the other. Just now he is in that house, the farmer's wife is ill. And there is only one man in the whole of Nexö who would be a better guide for you and that is Mr. Nielsen of the school. However, as you came that way you must have seen the rocking-stone."

We may have seen it, for we had seen stones galore.

A youngish man, tall and bare-headed, strode out of the farm-house. He was carrying a leather bag. His employé broke off the conversation with us and prepared to start the car which was decidedly antique.

The doctor told him they could wait a little, he was not in such a tearing hurry. Then he greeted us and said that he had always wanted to go tramping round the island, but he could not spare the time for it.

" They have been up to see the rocking-stone," remarked his man.

" Good, good ! " exclaimed the doctor. " You may not believe me, but I do assure you I have never seen it. Tell me, how were you impressed ? A strange thing, is it not ?

My friend the schoolmaster at Nexö says there is a fortress in this wild, uncultivated region. It is prehistoric. You will naturally ask why people should construct a fortress in a region such as that."

"It seems," I said, "a trifle odd, because it is a region nobody would want to capture."

"That is what I think, but Nielsen answers that it was a prehistoric fortress. Sometimes—you must really see him when you get to Nexö—sometimes he will talk about a little lake in there among the Hills."

"Is that a feature which one must have seen," I asked, "or be derided utterly?"

"Oh, not at all!" he cried. "In fact——"

"We will be very frank with you," said Petersen, "we have not seen the little lake."

Then did the physician burst into a shout of laughter. "Since it vanished many years ago, perhaps a million—that is what I hear from Nielsen——"

Petersen and I were looking virtuously at each other. We had been so truthful as regards the little lake. We told each other with a glance that there are times when one should not diverge from strict veracity. Suppose that, wanting to give pleasure to this man of Bornholm, we had praised the little lake, suppose that in the kindness of our hearts we had selected certain points for special approbation, such as the translucent magic of the water and the playful habits of the murderous, long fish, or the reflection of the budding elm-trees on the bank which had reminded us, we might have said, of tiny myriads of butterflies against the blackness of the twigs. Had we allowed ourselves to launch out in this fashion it would have been rather awkward to be told about the drying of the lake a million years ago. Decidedly there are occasions when one should be truthful.

"You would not demean yourselves," the doctor said, "to go by car, but may I take your rucksacks?" He had other patients to attend to on his round, he said, but if we would not walk too quickly he would be at the hotel before us.

It was most exhilarating not to have the rucksacks and Knut Petersen was very reasonable with regard to his prospective honeymoon, for he would have it somewhere else. Swiftly we proceeded, so that when the town came into sight below us and at no great distance it was necessary for us to delay, as otherwise we would be there before the doctor.

But it had been written that there would be a full hour's delay, because just at the entrance to the town there was a large, white building, one of those where fish are smoked. This factory—with several modest houses near it—fishermen's and market-gardeners', we ascertained—was in a stony, weed-grown space between the high road and the sea.

We were admitted to the spacious room in which the herrings were suspended over a great, fiery furnace, rows and rows of them. A man and several women were at work, to see that no untoward incident should mar the operation. While the man came up to us out of the smoke those women tended the long lines of scarlet flame.

One's thoughts flew to the worshippers who seek with sacrifice to win their gods' benevolence. All kinds of creatures—rams and ewes and goats and others—have been held to be appropriate. The gods have sometimes listened and have sometimes turned away. But is there any god who can resist the sacrifice of herrings? Talk of pleasant odours—is there one to equal herrings being smoked above a fire of wood? The nostrils of the gods will surely quiver and their hearts be melted when this lyric fragrance rises round them.

While the smoke prevented us from seeing very clearly I was under the impression that the faces of the man and women were serene, as if they knew that they need only pray and it would be fulfilled. But they were clothed in wisdom, they did not expect their gods to be particularly generous.

"I have to tell you," said the man, "that if you wish to eat some herrings they will not be ready till another hour has passed. They have to stay three hours in all." He recommended us to lie down in the grass beside the road and if we could, he said, it would be better not to think too much about the herrings, for we might be disappointed.

On the way to take up our positions in the grass we were debating whether he was right or whether one does not do well to dream and dream of future happiness, since one may never overtake it.

We determined, though, that we would pay this man the compliment of taking his advice. We probably would have been able to remain with minds content and blank, for a gay wind was blowing from the sea and there was such a merry dance of sunlight through the blue-gold halls of air and over the distracted waves of grass and on our eyes that we could scarcely keep them open.

Subsequently as we walked across the wind-blown space our host was warning us that on the table there would be no flowers. He had sent the children out for some when he espied us, but they might be unsuccessful. No, it was not right, he said, to let such people as ourselves sit down at a bare table. As for children, one could never know the way they would conduct themselves. He spoke apologetically, but there was a sort of twinkle in his voice.

Then I assured him we would not resent the absence of the flowers.

"But they would have shown," he said, "that we are civilized."

A scream rang out from somewhere and we saw the children, they were still a long way off and they were running frantically towards us.

"Oh, well," said their father, "they have not forgotten." Then he paid his tribute to them. "They are good, those children," he observed. "You see that market-garden just across the road? They might have broken in——"

There was a barbed-wire fence all round it.

"I am glad," I said, "they have not torn their clothes for our sake or got into trouble with the gardener."

"When he put the barbed-wire up I told my children that from now on they must know about the property of other people, that it is a wickedness to steal."

By this time those three flaxen-heads were not more than some eighty yards away. The wind was making it more difficult for them to run, but they were persevering nobly. As they plunged along we could not see what sort of flowers they had found, the gathering of which upon the stony beach had given them, we felt, such inconvenience. Those harassed, little faces looked to be aflame, the children were so breathless that we shouted at them, Petersen and I, to come more slowly.

"It is not much we can do for visitors," the parent said.

"The smallest one," said I, "is in a dreadful state. And if she comes a cropper on the stones——"

"Well, we are civilized," quoth he, "and strangers must be honoured."

Then we flung our arms around the staggering children, whose one thought was to confer on us the flowers. But alas, although these were the products of a hard and wind-swept soil, they had been here subjected to conditions they could not survive and they were moribund.

The children flushed still more, if possible, as we profusely thanked them and we all—the flowers excepted—were at peace with everybody as we crossed the threshold.

CHAPTER XI

OUR admirable host had warned us that we must not let our expectations be excessive and no doubt it is unwise always in the unknown to see splendour—*omne ignotum pro magnifico*, says Tacitus—but when at last they let us leave that hospitable house my sole regret was that the shoal of herrings we had eaten could not hear us while we sang their praises, one of us recalling with delight the texture, not too solid nor too flimsy, of their flesh, or we were eulogizing the aroma of them and their dusky gold appearance drove us to an outburst of enthusiasm.

Seeing that the master of the house where all this had occurred to us would not accept a penny, we decided that we would go back from Nexö with whatever we could buy for the three children and another one, the eldest girl who, like her father, hammered nails into the little wooden boxes after these had been so dexterously packed and salted by the women.

As we lay for a siesta on the beach it was enjoyable to gaze at the wide sheet of jewelled water that luxuriated with an indolence not less than ours; the wind had gone to sleep and you could hardly hear those timid wavelets kiss the land. And there it was that we received an embassy; those children, one could see from their demeanour, had in hand a matter of importance.

"Please take this," the eldest one announced, as she delivered to us each a box of herrings.

Then the younger children all explained, not very lucidly but in a kind of part-song, unrehearsed and lovely, that they had been sent to bring us these and that if we had not been lying there they would have followed us to Nexö and perhaps they never would have found us.

There are people who will ask impatiently why such an incident is here recorded. One should exercise, they will remind me, some discretion and refrain from having in a book, at any rate, all that which has no claim to be momentous. Be it so—and when I learn what things in life are unimportant I will say no more about them.

As the children had been told to come back after they had found us they were not quite sure if they could go to Nexö. It was a hard problem to decide, for if they consulted their own inclinations they would have escorted us. We pointed out that we were ignorant of Nexö, that it would be difficult for us to find a good confectioner and so they should not leave us in the lurch.

The youngest of the children clapped her hands.

"Of course," the eldest one said gravely, "we can walk home straight or not so straight—they did not tell us which we had to do."

The youngest one had placed her little hand in mine and

eloquently it was trembling. She and I set off in the direction of the town.

Her brother seized my other hand. " Well, I can show you, if you like," he said, " where the confectioner lives."

Behind us came the others.

I was a liner being towed into a port by two most energetic and efficient tugs. They would, I am convinced, have drawn me to my destination quite regardless of my own assistance or the lack of it.

We burst into the shop and very soon I ascertained that this confectioner was equal to the average—which is saying a great deal—in Denmark. One could take on board tremendous quantities of his ætherial merchandise and have no fear of foundering. I will admit that when the tugs had packed away in their respective holds much more than I could grapple with, a dread invaded me that in the end there would be a disaster. But when nothing of the sort occurred and I became, as time went on, less apprehensive, my prevailing sentiment was wonder mixed with homage, and I paid this tribute equally to the confectioner and to those who dealt so swiftly with his products.

The children could have reached their home without the slightest trace upon them of this expedition, for we wiped the sugar carefully from off the faces of the younger ones, but when we asked if they would like to carry back a parcel of some cakes and so on for the others they did not demur.

It was more difficult to find a toy-shop. Up and down those winding streets we wandered with the sandstone underfoot and the neat, many-coloured houses looking as if they were toys. At last we landed on a shop in which was an exiguous toy-department, but as there was nothing in it that our little friends appeared to disapprove of we were rather glad that it did not contain a larger stock.

Then they departed from us and we made our way to the hotel. I was reminded of a tale that you will know concerning an American who with his boy had gone into a London toy-shop for a Christmas present. The young woman who attended to them asked the boy if he would like an elephant on wheels and with a trunk to lift things up—

one had to wind the clockwork. But the boy said no, and he did not want soldiers, he was saying. When the girl put forward a suggestion of a drum he acquiesced immediately, and when his parent asked him what his brother and his sister would prefer he voted for a drum for each of them. The father gave the girl £2, because the drums cost thirty shillings. " Please excuse me," said the girl, " but are you an American ? " " That is so," said the man. " Have you been to the States ? " The girl said she had not, but she was interested for the reason that there was in her a little American. " Very good," the father said. " Pray keep the change and buy a drum for him."

At the hotel we found that not only had our luggage arrived, but as the porter solemnly was taking us upstairs we heard the voice of Mrs. Consul. She was in a room—the door was open—Captain Espersen was there, so was the landlord of the house, a tidy man with well-brushed hair, and a rubicund, small gentleman with a white, pointed beard. We were informed that he had lived for many years in South America and was revisiting his native place. He and the landlord had been schoolmates almost half a century ago.

" Who would have thought it," said the landlord, " that this fellow would go out and make a fortune ? "

" Not so vast a fortune," said the ruddy little man. " These other gentlemen may not have heard about our Andersen."

" Which Andersen ? We had at least a dozen of them."

" That is why he added Nexö to his name."

" Oh, that one," said the landlord. " Viggo Toxnoerd, you should know I do not read that sort of book."

Then Mr. Viggo told us that they two had been contemporaries at the school with Martin Andersen Nexö.

" I should like to know," the landlord said defiantly, " what he accomplished there."

" That does not matter," Mr. Viggo said. How would we like to see the house in which the great man used to live and on the way he would be telling us about him ?

So we sallied forth into the tranquil streets of Nexö, Mrs.

Consul, Captain Espersen and Petersen and I. There was time enough, said Mr. Viggo, for him to relate the story, seeing that the house which we were going to look at was a long way off, the last one of a certain road.

"We have been already," Mrs. Consul said, "and we know all about him, but one cannot hear it told too often."

Mr. Viggo then related that the family of Martin Andersen, his father and his grandfather, were from the neighbourhood of Nexö, but that when the boy was born, in 1869, they had removed to Copenhagen to a slum. The brothers and the sisters were extremely numerous. The father, when he was not drunk, would work upon the paving of the streets and frequently he thrashed the children. As a rule the mother was not in the house to intervene, for she was hawking fish to make a little money. Then it happened that they all went back to Bornholm—Martin was a lad of seven and he set to work beside his father in a quarry, while he spent the summer with the cattle in the fields. Later on he was apprenticed to a shoe-maker, but he was not robust, he found it very irksome to be kept away from the fresh air. While he was still a shoe-apprentice he was taken one day into Rönne, to a circle of good people who had literary tastes; they used to meet and lecture to each other. They perceived that there was something quite unusual in the boy, so they subscribed and, with the State assisting, he was able to go off to Jutland, to the well-known Askor High School. After that he was himself a teacher in the isle of Fyn, but this he had to give up owing to a weakness of the chest. A famous artist's widow paid for him to spend a year or so in Spain and Italy.

"I hope that woman lived to see him as a celebrated man," said Mrs. Consul.

Mr. Viggo did not know if she had been rewarded in that way. But she was wise, she thought the young man might be homesick and she would not let him have sufficient money to return to Denmark, not until he was in better health. And when he did come back he was a teacher at a private school in Copenhagen for the next few years.

We asked when he began to write and Mr. Viggo said that

he was rather late in starting. While he was a shoe-apprentice he had written a satiric poem on his master who had given him a thrashing, his first fee ; at Askor he occasionally wrote in local papers, afterwards he published several poems and short stories—full of sympathy with Nature and poor folk—but it was hard for him to settle on the form that suited him. It was in 1906 that he began his *Pelle the Conqueror*, a book which has been translated into seventeen languages. The first two parts—" I hope," said Mr. Viggo, " that I am not boring you. I am a worshipper."

We begged him to continue.

" Well, the first two parts of ' Pelle ' play in Bornholm. Pelle is a little shepherd and a shoe-assistant. How I envy you that you have not yet come across those books ! The other volumes, three and four, tell in a moving, very vivid fashion how the proletariat exist in Copenhagen. He has written other books and plays, but ' Pelle ' will in my opinion be regarded as his magnum opus. He shines most when he is dealing with the simple man, the man who fights against adversity. He has a rather wide horizon, wider than is usual with sociologists, and he has too much humour to be sentimental. He has been, and more than once, to Russia ; he admires profoundly what the Soviets are aiming at and for this reason many people here in Denmark, comfortable Denmark, were for quite a time disposed to look askance at our great citizen. And, by the way, he has a villa on a lake in Switzerland and there he is an honorary citizen. But now he lives near Copenhagen. I have been there twice," said Mr. Viggo. " It is wonderful to talk to him."

" What does he look like ? " asked Knut Petersen.

Mr. Viggo thought it over. " If I had to use one word," he said, " I would reply with leonine. And there," he said, " you have the house he lived in when he had to run down barefoot to the quarry. Some of us were jealous of him at the school because he told us that in summer he went up to the high meadows where he lay for hours and hours among his animals with nothing in the world to do."

"From time to time," said Mrs. Consul, "he would have to count them."

"I remember when we spoke of that," said Mr. Viggo, "and he told us that they answered to their names—of course they do. But when he told us one day that the clouds were singing as they sailed, we thought he had been overlong exposed to the hot sun. And, being boys, we told him what was in our minds."

"How did he explain himself?" asked Mrs. Consul. "One would like to know that very much."

"So far as I can recollect," said Mr. Viggo, "he said nothing."

We were opposite a very humble and dark-yellow house. Inside it there was emptiness, said Mr. Viggo, we had seen all that there was to see.

And, walking back with Mrs. Consul, I was told by her that she and Captain Espersen had separated after I had left them in the north-east of the island, separated owing to his military duties. Now it had been possible for him to spend a day or two at Nexö. She had known that he would come, to see the early home of one whose work he loved. That was a subject as to which their views were quite identical. And had I heard about that oak-tree and the beech near Svaneke, which are so intertwined that they are like two lovers? "They are very old," she said, "and they have scarcely reached a height of twenty feet. In August 1851 the King of Denmark had his name carved in the trunk, and that of the Queen as well. Nothing in the world," said Mrs. Consul, "can divide those two, and Espersen and I, we feel that we have been united by Andersen Nexö. From now on we will never part again."

I thought of asking her if they had not been ardent devotees of this good man when they were previously married. I was, like the Psalmist, disquieted within me. But perhaps, I thought, it would be better not to ask. There are so many questions that one cannot solve.

CHAPTER XII

PETERSEN did not like to go back and tell the lady that the first commission she had given him had ended in a failure and that he had not found any place appropriate for honeymoons among the Hills of Paradise. He therefore made enquiries of the landlord and the solemn porter and two or three of the Nexö shopkeepers with whom he conferred at considerable length, as a result of which he was provided with so much information that the lady would be able to pick and choose ; and he was in a state of such excitement to put all these facts before her that he could not wait another day. And after he had left that evening Mrs. Consul and her captain said that they had heard of a great walk by moonlight near the dunes. If I was not too weary they would be delighted . . .

Naturally I replied that I was very, very tired. And the invaluable hall-porter showed me on a map the route he had advised for them ; and there was quite another one, to Snogebæk, the Snake River, which he had reserved for me. He added that the dunes, at no great distance from the town, enjoyed a reputation.

" But you talk," I said, " as though you had not seen them for yourself."

" How can I ? " asked the man. " When I am old and pensioned I will have the leisure. Until then the dunes will have to wait for me. As for your friends, you will not incommode them, since the dunes are most extensive. And, besides, a person in them does not usually roam, because on such a surface of soft sand, not even level, it is a fatigue to walk." Let me go there, he said, and lie down in a sheltered spot, I would enjoy myself. And if I were to go astray among the dunes . . . He left the sentence incompleted.

" I suppose there are no savage beasts ? " I said.

"Down by the Laesaa Watercourse there are some ancient ones, quite ancient. I ought to have told you of them sooner."

"Now that I am warned," I said, "I will be ready for them. I have a good stick."

"Oho!" he laughed, "but they are not that kind of beast. A stick does not mean anything to them. They are the kind that one must look at."

I remembered some encounters with the dogs of Corinth, animals of gaunt pugnacity. When you have made it very plain to them that you do not propose to carry off a single sheep they are unwilling to believe you. In their eyes—ferocious, glittering eyes—the fact that you have moved away as rapidly as circumstances will permit does not mean that you can be trusted. They resemble many a successful man, for they are courageous and resourceful and unembarrassed by scruple; also they possess the splendid gift of concentration. They intend to put a stop to you, a final stop. Your sole defence is mesmerism, but that is not easy to apply when three of them advance on you from different quarters simultaneously.

"One has to look at them," I said, "as you were telling me."

"Look hard," he said, "for they are utterly unique."

"Yes," I agreed, "I never have been told of any others on the island. Can I not avoid that haunt of theirs, the Laesaa Watercourse?"

"You simply have to go there, everybody does." The fellow had a most determined air, as if he would brook no refusal.

"But a man like you," I said, "would surely never countenance bravado. And I think I would prefer a road not so encumbered with unpleasant brutes. I do profoundly hope my friends will not go in the wrong direction."

"But, sir"—he was speaking slowly and distinctly, as if to a backward child—"the beasts are very, very ancient. I have told you that."

"Their fangs may be more poisonous on that account," I said. "If I were a zoologist it would be different. Then it would be my duty to go down and watch them at the watercourse. They stay there, I presume?"

"God's Mother!" he expostulated, "they have stayed there for a thousand years, maybe for ten or twenty thousand or a million. Those animals are petrified. The scientists come here from a long way to study them."

I think I reeled a little. Why had he not said all this at once?

It happened just then, very luckily, that the proprietor came from his room. My second piece of fortune was that in my memory I had retained two words the porter had let fall. And as we went in the direction of the door I asked him if it was not rather odd for any Lutheran to say God's Mother—naturally I presumed the porter was a Lutheran.

"Now let me think a moment," said the landlord. "Yes, it was Lieutenant Anker. You may not have heard of him—one of our Bornholm heroes. When you are at Rönne go to the Museum, if you please, and you will find a portrait of him done in oils, a modest work of art, but he was a considerable hero. He was born near Rönne and in 1837, I believe, the son of a big farmer. He preferred the military life and after going through the college of cadets in Copenhagen he became a second-lieutenant of the Bornholm militia. He was living then at Rönne and he married."

"If," I said, "he was a born commander in the field he must have found it irksome to be stationed in this isle of peace."

"But you forget the war we had in 1864 against the Prussians and the Austrians. He was in the battle waged at Dübböl, the artillery was under him. Dübböl lay in Denmark, later on the German flag was over it and now it is again with us. So splendidly did Anker hold himself, encouraging his people gaily though it looked as though they would be overwhelmed, that he was honoured by the foe and in Berlin there is a monument commemorating Dübböl, with Lieutenant Anker shown in one of the reliefs. But what I want to tell you is about a letter you can see at the Museum. He was writing it when—if no reinforcements had appeared—he and his men were doomed.

'God's Mother'—that is what he wrote—'what will become of us?'"

A sojourner in Nexö might that evening have complained because her streets were somewhat destitute of animation. But there was great business in the sky. Although the moon could not stay long in any place it managed to illuminate the pale green dome with marvellous gold corridors of light. The moon would then have other work to do behind those heavy bosses on the dome and in the corridors much of the light would be extinguished.

Soon I had behind me the last house of Nexö and this would indeed have been an empty region if, a long way off, I had not seen the low, dark buildings of a farmstead. So the land was not a desolation, but as I strode on that farm exhibited a more and more inhospitable aspect, when the walls of it rose higher; but with not the slightest noise from man or beast and with no curl of smoke they might have been the walls of a plague-stricken, an abandoned place; and if there was a door or window I could not descry them. So my steps unconsciously were taking on a detour towards the left and presently from there I heard the faint and friendly lapping of the sea.

After the grim silence which enveloped all the land I was so much relieved that I could not help thinking of an episode in France with a most unresponsive lady at a dinner-table. Finally the man, when failure had attended all his efforts, asked her bluntly what she thought of incest. "Sir," she said, "I have to tell you I know nothing of it. I have always got on quite well with adultery."

There was the soothing murmur of the sea which, as I came in sight of it, was a broad shield of silvery-blue and it was being shaken. Nor was that the only sound which rose up to defeat the silence, for a lapwing—out, perhaps, to find provisions for his young—passed, a white and ghostly figure through the dimness. Fortunately he considered that his young or else the wanderlust or assignation, which at such an hour had sent him forth into the night, could wait a little; he descended and he came to rest on a convenient stone from which he weighed me up. However, it is possible his interest in me was mediocre and that his main object was to let me realize that he was a distinguished person with the black folds of his mantle beautifully speckled brown and white.

In due course I arrived at Snogebæk with the minutest harbour and its old-world storerooms where the fishing-gear is kept. A certain house, which otherwise was inconspicuous, proclaimed itself to be the meeting-place of a religious sect, one that does not believe in doing good by stealth, for in the kind of garden place and on the house itself were very large inscriptions in a minatory or triumphant language, to the end that all the folk of Snogebæk should walk in righteousness. It was surprising that such simple fishermen and farmers had to have these drastic methods brought to bear upon them.

One Snogebækian, a grizzled fellow, stepped out of a wooden cabin, evidently made of driftwood, and surveyed the sky.

"Good night," I said to him.

"And we will have good fishing," he replied.

I mentioned that I had been reading those inscriptions on the house and the adjacent walls.

He nodded.

"But one does not find them everywhere. Do you approve of them?" I asked.

"Why not?" said he. And then he started to fill up his pipe as though there was no more to add. "But come into my house," said he, "and have an acquavit or two. The night is cold."

He struck a match as we went in. The moonlight would, he said, not be sufficient, as he had all his belongings there and I would knock myself on some of them. Also he would like to tell me that his name was Jesper Lund.

It would be impossible to give a catalogue of what the lamp revealed . . . there was a table with no cloth upon it in the middle of the room, a part of it was given over to the relics of a meal or preparations for the next one, butter in an open tin, a slab of very yellow cheese, cold bacon and a loaf of brown bread. I could not examine all the room, the fishing-nets and so forth, in a detailed fashion, as my host was handing me the acquavit. When I had tossed it off I knew that Fate had meant us two to come together, when I drank another one I wanted very much to shout this knowledge to the world and when another glass had been absorbed I had an urgent longing to walk with him through the night, but not to walk, I must have races with the wind.

How could I, being occupied in this way, peer into the crannies of that room which answered all the needs of day and night?—my gaze was caught by two things in the miscellaneous multitude: a pair of well-oiled sea-boots lay upon the table and there was a shelf of books.

"Oh yes," he said, "one reads a little, but the man for that is Peter Thorsen of Peterskir. He is—well, I have heard him called a museum-piece. And the learned men from Sweden and from Copenhagen come to ask him questions. Do you mean to say you have not planned to visit him? He is not far away—just over there at Peterskir."

I thought it best not to expose my ignorance. And so I waited in the hope that Mr. Lund would carry on.

"You surely must know something of our greatest man," he said. "His fame has penetrated everywhere."

"The least that one can do," said I, as I poured out the acquavit, "is for us two to drink his health."

When this had ceremoniously been accomplished Mr. Lund, while not exactly mellowing, was in a more indulgent frame of mind. He shut his eye to my deficiencies and, speaking figuratively, danced before the shrine of Peter Thorsen.

"Such a man!" he cried. "A farmer not more prosperous than the average, his investigations into other fields have been remarkable. That theory he put forward as to why the primitive inhabitants carved circles on a stone, it is a theory which the Scandinavian men of science have accepted with enthusiasm. Peter Thorsen always pointed out that he did not look on those early people as indecent only when they drew the circles. I, of course," said Mr. Lund, "I am as nothing when compared with him, but

I believe he says that they had other and quite noble thoughts."

A picture hung beside the door, it was a print in a black wooden frame, the full-face portrait of a man with no outstanding features. He was middle-aged and melancholy. Was this, I wondered, Peter Thorsen, taken at a time when someone had objected to his theory?

"I can see what you are looking at," said Mr. Lund. "I hang it there, as far away as I can put it from the stove. I want to keep the smuts away from it."

"You reverence that man," I said.

"Assuredly," said Mr. Lund. "He is the President of the Association of Teetotallers."

"But you," I said, "are not a member of it, not an active member?"

"Does one not do well," asked Mr. Lund, "to be a man of tolerance and to respect the other side? But we were talking about Peter Thorsen. And what books he has in several languages and the transactions of societies in England and America and other places! He subscribes to those and reads them for his pleasure, though he is a simple countryman. Sometimes he will do an article himself and I have seen them printed with his name in very serious kinds of papers."

"Have you not a portrait of this man?" I asked. "It seems to me that you admire him even more than the teetotaller."

Alas, said Mr. Lund, he had no portrait, but he could explain to me what Thorsen looked like—a grey-headed, kindly sort of man with a grand forehead and with eyes . . . "Well, I could say," said Mr. Lund, "that they are like the sunlight falling out of a blue sky, you understand? And now, if you are ready, we can go."

He blew the lamp out, and as we went from the cabin I perceived that nearly all the clouds had disappeared. And from the primrose-coloured vault that was so like a song of angels, from a point of it the moon was pouring splendour. I strode on, with Mr. Lund beside me. We were making for those hillocks of pale sand, the dunes, and they were so distinct in that mysterious light that one could see the scanty tufts of greenery among them. Everything was clearer than is usual, except why Mr. Lund was walking with me. He was obstinately silent as we tramped beside the sea. From time to time I glanced at him and saw that he was agitated to the depths.

Suddenly he spoke: " The heaviest burden for a traveller," he said, " is a light purse."

" Nevertheless . . ." I started to reply.

" But one may have a heavier burden still," he said.

To walk on was great weariness, but I had to remain with Mr. Lund. I wondered if he made a practice of perambulating to and fro upon these heart-break dunes, for he did not seem to be troubled by them. Very possibly he was so plunged in wretchedness of mind that he was unaware of what was happening to his body.

Then a groan escaped me, I was in a whirlpool of fatigue.

" How good of you," said Mr. Lund, " to sorrow for me. It is good of you."

" One cannot walk," I said, " and weep. Let us sit down." And then I asked if there was anything that I could do.

With startling brusqueness he began. " From that direction "—he was pointing to the north—" those Swedish vessels came—oh, long ago. We were at war with Sweden then, but what is that to you ? "

I begged him to go on. It interested me, I said, immeasurably. If he would tell me a long tale, I thought, of an obscure engagement, it might be a little drab for me to listen to, but much more pleasant than the sorrow which was gnawing at his heart.

" From that side they came," he said, " and Wrangel was the admiral. But wars were different from to-day. The Swedish boats were anchored on account of the unfavourable winds, the men on board were fishing and they did no injury to Snogebæk or Nexö. Well, the admiral had a good eye for profit, so he brought a little ship from Pomerania, full of merchandise, his private property. He would do business with the men of Nexö. But the crew began to quarrel with the fishermen and so they captured butter, chickens, ducks and lambs and probably some other things."

"How well informed you are," I said.

"It was in '44, in 1644," said Mr. Lund, "and then at night the men of Nexö, on a darker night than this, rowed out and seized that boat from Pomerania and pulled it into harbour and divided for the general good all that was in it. So the admiral swore loudly he would be revenged and in the next year he came with a fleet of twenty-nine and he directed a great fire upon the town. He landed, not at Snogebæk, at Nexö, and he told his men that they could plunder it for several hours. Three merchants only had their houses spared. Ah, those were days! But now—now——"

"Will you tell me why he spared those three?" I asked.

"He wanted to do business with them."

Mr. Lund was now in a more tranquil frame of mind, although the story of that overwhelming sorrow still had to be told. I might have risen, muttered an excuse and a farewell and then have hurriedly departed. But I could not leave the poor old man.

"Those were the days," he sighed.

A few stars were now visible. "Of course," I said, "it is a callous thing to tell a person that his grief will vanish. And yet it is true. Look at the stars."

"I know them well," he said. "I am a sailor. That one is Orion, that one on the right——"

"But what of those you cannot see, those which are dead? Your sorrow, it will vanish like the stars. Dear Mr. Lund, there was a time when those, the dead ones, were as brilliant as the others and they were like golden nails that could be driven into you. The sorrows that you have to-day will vanish in their own good time, so why not treat them as if they had faded out already?"

He was rubbing one gnarled hand upon the other. "I have known the stars for many, many years," he said, "and I have never seen one die."

"The people who concern themselves with such affairs,"

I said, "have told us that the dying of a star, when it becomes a cold, dark body, happens over a long period of centuries."

He put his hand upon my shoulder, he was smiling furtively. "You promised me about my sorrow, it would vanish like the stars," he said, "but that is a long time to wait." He told me then that he was the possessor of a very ancient boat and of a newer one. That was the trouble.

"You hesitate," I said, "about demolishing the old one?"

"So far I have left it," answered Mr. Lund, "upon the shore, and every day when I return it has a look of utter loneliness. It wears me out to see the poor thing's misery."

"If one is merciful," I said, "one puts out of his misery an aged and beloved dog. As for a boat . . ."

"It is like this," he said. "I come back from the fishing, there she lies upon the shingle. How we lived together in the bygone days, scene after scene of it returns. We used to put to sea when others did not dare. I can remember times when she would ride at ease upon the roaring waves. So purple they would be in anger, white foam battered from the rocks—my friends were on them, wondering when we would be destroyed. And then the quiet mornings when the sun—how shall I tell you?—lays a sweetly-coloured carpet on the sea and God walks over it. What have we not been through together?"

"When your ancestors," I said, "the Vikings, made a funeral pyre, the dead man and the long-ship blazing as they floated on the water, I am certain that they had a great affection for the ship as well."

He nodded gravely. "I have heard," he said, "about those Vikings. I have seen a picture of one after he was dead and, as you say, the boat and he were all aflame."

"A splendid way of passing out," I said.

"It is indeed," said Mr. Lund. "If I could go like that! Will you—no, you will not be here to have it done and I do not believe the pastor would allow it."

Nowadays, I said, one had to burn the ship alone, with no dead warrior lying in it. Noble ships, I said, deserve to have that glorious end. And was not his beloved boat as meritorious as a long-ship of the Vikings? They were instruments of war, but his brought nourishment for many people from the sea. No honour we could pay would be excessive.

"So you mean," said Mr. Lund—his voice was husky with emotion—" that we should commit her to the flames? I sometimes "—he was whispering now—" have thought of it."

"To-night," I said, " it is propitious."

"That is true," said Mr. Lund.

Without another word we rose and started back upon the moonlit shore. No longer did I find it arduous to walk on that unstable sand, for now we were engaged in an exalted and a hallowed enterprise.

And thus we came to Snogebæk.

"What do you think?" said Mr. Lund. "A bottle of some wine is broken on a ship when she goes down into the water. Well now, when she goes down for the last time . . ."

"I have never heard," I said, " of such a celebration then."

"You may be right," said Mr. Lund. "So let us go into the house and drink a little, you and I."

On this occasion and to put us, Mr. Lund said, in the proper mood, we were quaffing acquavit and beer alternately. And in the course of our potations we were uttering a speech or two, that is to say my colleague started in a seemly fashion to explain that this was most significant. I waited for him to continue, but as he said nothing more just then I thought it would be opportune for me, in my turn, to begin a speech. And so I said that it was a high privilege for me to take a part in such proceedings, venerable to the point of—I was weighing in my mind what next to say, but as I settled Mr. Lund began again and thus we made two simultaneous speeches. It is undeniable that there are disadvantages in such a method, but it saves a lot of time.

Some people, having taken part in that kind of a

duologue, would frown at one another. We did not. In perfect amity we issued from the house and arm-in-arm negotiated the short distance to the boat, lying as she was about half-way between the house and her old element.

A clumsy craft she seemed to me, whatever pulchritude she might possess upon the water.

" How shall we begin ? " asked Mr. Lund.

Well, I have in my time committed many things, but never had I contemplated setting fire to any ship and so I had no theories on the subject. We considered that her fishy state would render her inflammable, though not perhaps to the required degree. It would be very morbid if the conflagration peter out and leave the charred remainder of her rocking woefully upon the water.

Mr. Lund said that he had discovered in a book or magazine about some Asiatic bandits who were kneeling down in a long row to have their heads cut off. The executioner was efficacious for the first three culprits, as he gave one blow to each of them. But on arriving at the fourth he bungled in a very amateurish fashion, only getting half-way through the victim's neck. Thereupon the dignitary who presided over the affair was much incensed, the more so since some foreigners, Americans and British, were the guests of honour. Then he called on the assistant-executioner to show his comrade how the task should be accomplished; he was told to chop off all the other heads and to begin with that one which belongs—so said the dignitary—to your senior and erring partner. One should take the strongest measures, should one not, quoth Mr. Lund, against an executioner who does not execute completely ?

It was gratifying for me, I remarked, to be in a position to support the case with further testimony from abroad. There should be no doubt at all about the person's death. When somebody is murdered in Andorra three important men of the republic march up to the corpse and they address it. " Corpse," they exclaim, " arise, considering that justice does demand it of thee ! " If he fails to do so one presumes that he is dead.

"It seems to me," said Mr. Lund, "that your example, though I like it, is not very good. What were the steps the Vikings took so that the long-ships should be burned completely? Did they pour in a supply of oil?"

"Who knows?" I said. "But if you have some oil yourself . . ."

"Oh yes," he answered, "for I have an engine in my other boat. Wait here a little." Then he ran up to the house again and presently returned with a red metal can.

We emptied it into the ship, we placed the wooden runners underneath the keel, we pulled and pushed and soon she was afloat, with us at either side, the water gently lapping round our legs. The wind was very slight and so irregular that one could not be certain if she would be carried out to sea. We hoisted the main-sail, we tied the tackle in the manner that seemed opportune to Mr. Lund, and then we only had to set the oil alight and hope that everything would turn out well.

Mr. Lund leaned on the boat. "I never in my life," he said, "have felt like this, not when a friend of mine has died."

"And I should be astonished if you ever have performed," I said, "a nobler action. Think how you release the boat from all her misery. She will be sailing out to where . . . in fine, to where . . ."

"Do you believe," asked Mr. Lund, "that she and I will meet again?"

"I do not know," I said, "if such a boat as this one, which has braved so many storms, I do not know if she will be content at first to be admitted to the stormless region."

"She is old," said Mr. Lund. He bent down and he splashed some of the oil on to the flapping sail. After that he struck a match; he let it fall into the bottom of the boat. A bluish flame was leaping upward, but not high enough to reach the sail. However it was then the sail gave her assistance, for she curtsied towards the blaze and into it. So there sprang up such wreaths of brilliant and fantastic flowers that very soon the battered fishing-boat had the appearance of the loveliest of gardens.

"Now!" said Mr. Lund.

If there had arisen a kind breeze to blow the burning vessel from the shore it would have been in every way less disagreeable for us. We would have preferred to stand immovable and watch the poor old ship sail out on her last journey; having to collaborate and push her on the road caused us to feel too much like executioners. It also was becoming every moment far more perilous to touch the stricken hull. But, very fortunately, as with all our strength we thrust her from us, she was taken by a current and she glided out beyond our reach. By this time she was thoroughly in the possession of the flames, which made it probable that she would meet her death, not ignominiously upon the beach, but in the old-time, splendid way, reclining on the water.

Then a flock of sea-gulls whirled about the blazing ship. They called and called, as if they were the heralds making their announcements to the sea and air and sky. Perhaps it was a threnody which they were singing. And perhaps it was a song of exultation that the Vikings had returned. They knew—for it is handed down from sea-gull unto sea-gull—how the water-burial was conducted in those distant days. Themselves they have not swerved from the beloved, beautiful traditions; now it seemed that man was willing to acknowledge, after the misguided centuries, that he should not have cast aside the customs of his ancestors. Whatever may have been the burden of the sea-gulls' song, the mood which they were in was more than usually abandoned; with a reckless rush they circled not so far above the flames and through the smoke. Their bodies, dazzling in the moonlight, were converted each time by the smoke into the colour of old ivory.

And so with an aerial escort the fiercely-burning ship went on her way.

The moon was clothed in radiance and serenely sat enthroned upon a sapphire carpet. She was holding a review of the battalions of the sky. Dark regiments rode past the point where she was stationed; now and then there was a break between the ranks, the moon would lay her golden hand upon a straggler to encourage him. The ranks would form again, so massive that the moon was all obscured and they would hurry onward to their unknown destination.

CHAPTER XIII

ALL that morning Mrs. Consul went about in the hotel and in the streets of Nexö with a telegram in her left hand. I was told the contents of it as we met upon the stairs and I have little doubt that a good many of the citizens of Nexö, wondering what could be in the telegram to make the lady stride along in such exhilaration, were immediately informed by her that there was not a happier woman in the whole of Denmark or the world.

I was with her in the market-place and there she noticed Mr. Viggo, who was stroking his white beard in front of one of those small, temporary shops with canvas walls.

Mrs. Consul asked at once if he could spare a moment. He remembered, did he not, from yesterday that she was married to a man who was entrusted with the interests of Nicaragua? Now she would like to talk to Mr. Viggo on the subject of the Nicaraguan navy.

Then his rosy face grew rosier. " I can see," he said, " that it has had a victory. May I congratulate? How did they do it? Long live Nicaragua!"

" My husband, my dear husband could not ascertain," she told him, " if they have a navy, battleships, you know, and submarines and so forth. But if they have none of them they will have a merchant-navy, will they not?, because they have a coast-line—I have seen it on the map— and now and then a Nicaraguan seaman would do like the men from other countries and would go to see his Consul."

Through the years that Mr. Viggo had been as a businessman in Buenos Aires he had never been concerned with Nicaragua. But he was anxious to be helpful and he was now less entirely in the dark than when the conversation had begun, for he had learned that Nicaragua has a coast. He suggested that it would be nice if they could have a little talk where it was not so crowded; as he gently laid his hand upon her arm he steered her through the market-place.

"And here," he said, "here we can seat ourselves in comfort. Yes, I am quite sure that there are Nicaraguan seamen. At this moment I would not be able to inform you what the numbers are, but——"

"If there is one man, that is enough," she cried. "And do you think God has bestowed a Nicaraguan seaman on my husband? No other Nicaraguan would have recourse to him. I so devoutly hope for it, because he is the best of men, the best of consuls. In this telegram—no, I can stay no longer, I am so excited—in this telegram he says that he will put no obstacle to our divorce and then I shall be free to have the captain and he says that he is sorry not to be with us, but he is busy. There has never been a more deserving man and I would be more glad than I can say if he is busy with a Nicaraguan seaman."

"It is possible," said Mr. Viggo, "that there are quite a number of them."

"Thank you, thank you," she exclaimed. And as we proceeded to the public garden she was telling me that she was overjoyed because of the fair tidings which she had obtained from Mr. Viggo. "I have always held," she said, "that God is full of kindliness."

I told her that in England we have people so misguided as to think that when the letters D.G.—Dei Gratia—had been omitted from the coinage, some ninety or a hundred years ago, the country had in consequence an outbreak of cholera. But later on those letters were restored.

"You have to be polite," said Mrs. Consul. "So goodbye. Now I must hurry on."

The landlord had considered it appropriate that there

should be a re-betrothal lunch; the others—murmuring good wishes—hovered round us while we ate: the stocky waiter with his pince-nez, the assistant-waiter trying not to show that this was one of the red-letter days of his young life and our good friend the solemn porter who looked in from time to time. If the landlord and the cook had had more opportunity to think it out the menu would, I daresay, have been somewhat different, it might even—God forbid—have been more ample. What we had in front of us had been entirely improvised that morning when the landlord heard our jocund news. We had honoured him with our betrothal and the lunch was on the house. Mr. Viggo had been summoned too.

"Was it not kind of him," said Mrs. Consul as she helped herself to the grilled mussels with the curry mayonnaise, "to spend his money on a telegram?"

Captain Espersen was hesitating, for the liver-paste with a meat jelly and the roast duckling with cucumber salad looked equally attractive. With his fork, although some of the duckling was transfixed upon it, he performed a graceful movement in the air. "He is a man," the captain said, "whom I respect. I trust that in the years to come——"

"My love," said Mrs. Consul, "what we ought to do is to provide him with another wife. I am relieved that you are serving now in Copenhagen. It will not be long before we find him something suitable. Give me a little of that beef marrow on the toasted rye bread."

"All that I can do," the captain said, "I will do. He must come to Copenhagen after we have picked the lady."

"The dear man," said Mrs. Consul. "I shall be exacting, most exacting, let me warn you."

"He will have to stay with us," said Captain Espersen.

"And we will have the wedding in our house," said Mrs. Consul. "But I think we cannot, for he likes to have his weddings in a church."

Then it was necessary, in the landlord's presence, to pay serious attention to the food. Yes, he said, they both would please us—those anchovies in their oyster sauce with the chopped egg and capers or those cakes of fried forcemeat with red cabbage.

"Now," said the landlord, "what I have to do is to felicitate the couple. May you——"

It was arduous but, notwithstanding, we pushed back the chairs and struggled to our feet.

"Oh, let me beg you," said the landlord, "but the cook would never be the same glad cook again if you do not do justice to that dish of poached eggs in the company of mushrooms, truffles and fresh lobster, prettily encamped on toast. Well, I rely on you. And as for me, I am not skilful at orations. But the fact will always be that if a custom has been kept for many years—and yet a custom is not merely good because of age."

That was an opportunity presented on a silver plate. I had a tale whose telling would enable me, whatever it might do for my companions, to cry off awhile in my attack upon the good things of the table. So I told them of an ancient family in France, that of the Dukes of Levis-Mirepoix. One of their predecessors had a piece of mediæval tapestry whereon he was depicted with the Blessed Virgin and the Child. Some words, embroidered neatly, issue from the Virgin's lips as she is turning to the Duke. "I beg you," she is saying, "to keep on your hat, my cousin."

"That is wonderful indeed," observed the landlord.

"Wonderful," agreed the waiter, staring at us through his pince-nez very earnestly, "and we have no one like a duke in Bornholm. Formerly," he said, "who knows——"

Then I continued. There had been, I told them, a descendant of that Duke, a personage who held himself and his nobility in high esteem. Some fifty years ago he happened to be sitting in his club down at Toulouse; a member, who pretended not to know him, asked in a stage-whisper that was audible to everybody in the room: "Who is yonder gentleman, the one who has a velvet collar to his coat?" "How is it possible you do not know?" the other member said. "That is the Duke of Levis-Mirepoix." "And is he," asked the first one, "is he of a decent family?"

We managed to make several interruptions into the tremendous hospitality of Nexö, so that the re-betrothal lunch became prolonged. And we were all so friendly that the landlord said that he could not believe that yesterday we had been strangers.

"Let me tell you of that man," said Mr. Viggo, "who was drunk a little, it was in the night. He met a person who was also partly drunk. 'Excuse me,' said the first one, 'but is that the sun up there or else the moon?' 'I cannot tell you,' said the other one, 'I am a stranger here.'"

"I am very satisfied with everything," the captain said, "and so I can go back to Rönne."

"You," I said, "are to be envied, for you have a task, you do it and you are not worried with the thought of the loose ends you leave, of something you have left undone."

"I have examined all the young men and the horses and the guns. But I can also find the time for other things."

Mrs. Consul laid her hand on his.

"The other day," said he, "I happened to be browsing in the memoirs of Madame Arman de Caillavet. An early friend of hers, the Captain Rivière, who was well known in his day both as a naval officer and as a novelist, wrote in a letter to the lady that there are no different countries, there is only the small creature which is oneself, always the same and which, wherever it is, wants to eat, drink, sleep and make love from time to time and, when it has the leisure, to use its intelligence. When a person, quoth Rivière, can do all that he is like the philosopher Bias, he carries the world about with him."

"Is that," asked Mrs. Consul, "the same Madame de Caillavet who——?"

"Yes, it was she," said Espersen, "whose most illustrious friend was Anatole France and during the twenty most fruitful years of his life. An hour or two after she had passed away he wrote to Dr. Aunis 'My life is at an end' and in another letter he wrote that 'Her death is my death.'"

"But as he was also a philosopher," said Mrs. Consul, "it will have helped him to bear the blow."

The landlord had to answer someone on the telephone. As he got up he said he must confess he did not know that Bias they were talking of. Was he a man about whom one should know?

"Maybe," said Espersen, "but personally I am interested more in Anatole France, the sceptic who was so serene. Some people looked askance upon him when he had installed in his own house Madame de Caillavet's second housemaid to be his mistress, others looked upon it as a very touching demonstration."

Presently we said farewell to the kind landlord and the staff; and slowly, sadly we proceeded to the station. You are quite at liberty in Bornholm to go promenading up and down a railway platform whether you propose to patronize the line or not. Two singularly handsome carriages were having their blue panels washed, although one would not have supposed that it was needed. Each of them contained accommodation, charming and luxurious, for twenty passengers, and as it only takes about an hour to get to Rönne one must give the railway company full marks.

"I do not know," said Mrs. Consul, "but it may be to avoid an anti-climax. After the fine scenery upon the coast, those Hills of Paradise and so on we might be extremely mournful to be looking at the meadow-land which, for the most part, is the kind of country we shall see, I think. And so they tempt the passengers to gaze admiringly round this compartment and when they have finished their inspection, lo! they are in Rönne."

We strolled along the platform, out beyond it on the sandy surface. When we had again approached the station we were courteously accosted by a porter. There was time enough, he said, for us to make a little expedition to the church—he would point out the way—and there was in the churchyard—we would find it easily—a beautiful, red sandstone monument, not large, but very old and beautiful. He would be very sorry if we were to leave without a glimpse of it.

"That man reminds me of the day," said Captain Espersen, "when most of Bornholm was in Swedish hands.

The blue and yellow of the flag of Sweden—have you ever seen more primrose-coloured hair?—and his blue eyes are so disarming."

The church was locked, but when we looked in through the plain glass windows there did not seem to be anything which had to be examined closely.

Very soon we found the sandstone carving. It was obviously the work of one whose technical accomplishment fell short of his artistic dream. The face in profile of a child was indicated rather than completed. Yet I shall be sorry for the person who does not behold the pathos of it and the loveliness of things that pass away.

As we looked in silence we were interrupted by the sound of steps upon the gravel and the porter was explaining why he had resolved to follow us. We might be there at the memorial so long, he said, that it would make us miss the train. However we could tarry for awhile and he stood there with us in contemplation. Then he spoke, addressing no one in particular. "If it is better to die young," said he, "or not to die?

'Maidenhood, maidenhood mine, must I call you in vain?
Yours never again, yours never again, yours never again.'"

"Those words," said Espersen, "of Sappho's are in my opinion the most tragic that she wrote and the most beautiful."

"Shall we go back now to the station?" said the porter.

He and Espersen strode side by side; I could not hear what they were talking of. I wish I could have spent more time with both of them.

A whistle rang out from the station, but our friend the porter turned and made a gesture with his hands; the meaning of it was that we could still continue calmly.

"So this expedition will be coming to an end," said Mrs. Consul. "I have reason to remember it with gratitude, for it has brought the captain back to me. But I am not entirely selfish, I have thought of you"—she looked at me —"from time to time. You have not been held up for a heavy ransom by the bandits, whose nocturnal relaxation was to chant the stirring folk-songs (see appendix)—you permitted by their courtesy to take part in the chorus ; you have not run helter-skelter with an earthquake tearing up the ground behind you, so that you have only just been able to escape ; you have not found yourself upon a narrow bridge with a most savage creature that you had perforce to strangle and you did not, when you woke up to discover that your hosts were anthropophagous, you did not cause them to enrol themselves in the Salvation Army and forthwith to celebrate a week of self-denial. You have not, in fine, had numerous adventures. No, not even have you camped out underneath the moon, when it is noxious insects and not sleep, in my experience, which falls from off the trees."

"We have not scorned hotels," I said, "and lived laborious nights."

This time the locomotive blew with more insistence and we had to hurry to the station.